Hamlyn all-colour paperbacks

Plantagenet Somerset Fry
F.R.S.A.

Antique Furniture

illustrated by John W. Wood and Associates

Hamlyn - London
Sun Books - Melbourne

FOREWORD

This is a history of 4000 years or more of domestic furniture. Possibly it is the shortest book on the subject ever written. It may therefore be wondered why about a quarter of the text is devoted to one century of furniture from one country, France.

I make no apology for this imbalance. Furniture can satisfy several needs; decoration, use, comfort, aestheticism. In my view – and I am not alone in it – French furniture of the 18th century represents the highest achievement in the whole history of the craft, and it satisfies all four needs to a far greater degree than any furniture before or since. Many of the cabinet-makers' pieces are breath-taking to look at, a positive joy to use.

In expressing this view, I do not overlook the styles of other lands, many of which are extremely fine and pleasing, particularly those of Georgian and Regency England, Dutch Baroque and American Chippendale, to mention but a few.

To prepare this book I have drawn upon the considerable literature on the subject, some volumes of which are listed on page 156 and to whose authors I am much indebted. I am also extremely grateful to Miss Gillian Wilson, of the Department of Education and Science, for valuable assistance on the chapters which discuss French 18th-century furniture. Lastly, I owe my wife a debt for reviving my interest in antique furniture after it had evaporated following a great personal loss.

PLANTAGENET SOMERSET FRY

(front cover illustration) Mid 18th-century small commode with lacquer *Chinoiserie* decoration, probably by J. Dubois
(back cover illustration) Armchair from a set of eight George III armchairs, in mahogany with inlay of different woods, about 1785

Published by the Hamlyn Publishing Group Limited
London · New York · Sydney · Toronto
Hamlyn House, Feltham, Middlesex, England
In association with Sun Books Pty Ltd Melbourne

Reprinted 1972

ISBN 0 600 00141 5
Phototypeset by Filmtype Services Limited, Scarborough
Colour separations by Schwitter Limited, Zurich
Printed in Holland by Senefelder, Purmerend

CONTENTS

THE ANCIENT WORLD

Egypt

The ancient Egyptians believed that when a pharaoh died his soul continued in a life after death. This was only possible if the pharaoh's body was embalmed and placed in a tomb which was then hermetically sealed. The first such tombs were the pyramids, erected during the Old Kingdom dynasties (c.2800–c.2300 BC). Later on, pharaohs were embalmed and buried in huge graves hewn out of rocks.

As the body of the pharaoh was being preserved in order to facilitate his transference to the after-life, it was also considered important that he should take with him all those comforts he had enjoyed on earth. Thus arose the custom of surrounding the pharaoh's body, which was sometimes put in a sarcophagus, with a variety of precious jewels, weapons, household utensils, food and other domestic paraphernalia. Among these were items of furniture – not only those used by the pharaoh but also some pieces used by his family or attendants – and it is due to the efficacy of ancient Egyptian tomb-sealing that today we can see many of these pieces in an excellent

(*right*) Upright chair of cedar-wood with gold mounts. This was found in the tomb of the pharaoh Tutankhamen and is now in the Egyptian Museum, Cairo. Some decorated strutwork is missing from between the seat and the stretchers

(*far right*) Box mounted on square legs. The framework is ebony and the lid is mounted on bronze hinges. From Tutankhamen's tomb

state of preservation. Some of the wood and the leather upholstery appear to be in as good a condition as they were when entombed thousands of years ago.

These, and other surviving Egyptian items, are the oldest pieces of furniture in the world. They date, at the earliest, from about 1500 BC, that is, in the New Kingdom dynasties, shortly after the expulsion from Egypt of the Hyksos by Ahmose I. But from ivory carvings of the Old Kingdom it is clear that wooden furniture was being made at least eight hundred years earlier. What is more, the types of furniture and the manner in which they were made had hardly changed in all those years.

Throughout its long history Egyptian furniture appears to have been simple in design and practical in use, although some pieces made especially for pharaohs were more refined,

Folding stool of cedarwood, about 1500 BC. The inlay is ivory and the legs have ducks' head ends. This stool is now in the British Museum, London

with elaborate ivory and ebony inlays. When in 1922 the tomb of the pharaoh Tutankhamen was discovered and opened up by the archaeologists the Earl of Caernarvon and Howard Carter, a variety of pieces of furniture was found in the antechamber. Some were heavily ornate, others were in a much simpler style. The chair shown here is far less elaborate than the more famous ecclesiastical throne which has, apart from ivory and ebony, overlays of gold, glass and semi-precious stones.

In Egypt there was always a shortage of strong indigenous woods, for palm-tree wood was far too unstable for solid stress-bearing furniture. The Egyptians therefore had to import cedarwood, sycamore and olivewood from the Lebanon and Cilicia. They also imported ebony and ivory from areas further south on the African continent.

Egyptian carpenters had at their disposal a variety of tools: saws with bronze blades, chisels, mallets, axes and sharp knives. Planes had not yet been invented and adzes were used for smoothing surfaces. They also developed many cabinet-making techniques which have persisted throughout the history of furniture. They knew the art of making strong lasting glues. They made joints between members by mortise and tenon, and they developed skilful dovetailing. They made bronze hinges for chest or box lids, and they upholstered chairs, stools and beds with leather strapping, plant-fibre and cloth.

The main pieces of furniture made by the Egyptians were chairs (thrones and other styles), stools, beds, chests and caskets. The Egyptian chair usually had a square seat on carved wood animal legs, all four legs facing forwards, with a curved sloping back supported by perpendicular stretchers. The seat was made of plaited leather straps or rushes beaten into strong fibrous strips, nailed at the sides.

Another item which was introduced during the Middle Kingdom dynasties (c.2200–c.1800 BC) was the folding stool. The seat of this collapsible stool consisted of either a row of leather straps nailed or glued from rail to rail, or a piece of draped leather sewn into right angles at the corners, which was detachable. The legs often ended in carved ducks' heads, inlaid with ivory. These stools were used domestically and also by army commanders in the field of battle.

The ancient Egyptians appear to have invented the bed, and several examples have survived, some of which are in very good condition. The one found in the tomb of the architect Cha at Thebes is typical. (Important people other than pharaohs were sometimes buried in great tombs, along with their worldly goods.) Like the chairs the legs of beds all face in the same direction. What appears to be the headboard, however, is in fact a footboard. The head rested either on pillows or on a special headrest of wood, which was a separate piece of furniture. The frame of the bed was filled with a network of leather or plant-fibre.

Egyptian bed, of the 16th century BC, found in the tomb of the architect, Cha, at Thebes. It is probably of cedar, painted white

Assyria and Persia

There are no surviving pieces of furniture from those two splendid Near-Eastern empires, Assyria and ancient Persia. All that is known of their furniture comes from such sculpture and stone reliefs as have been excavated in the past hundred years or so, many of which were found in the ruins of palaces of Assyrian and Persian kings. Most of the items depicted are associated with regal or religious ceremonial, military campaigning, or life at the court of an omnipotent ruler.

A typical Assyrian chair was high-backed, perpendicular and with the seat raised so high above the ground that a separate footstool was needed. This type of chair appears to have been made deliberately to emphasize the superiority of the sitter over other people in the same room, and was used by kings and high priests. Although the chair in the illustration has no animal feet, the square legs of many Assyrian chairs did end in lions' paws, in the Egyptian manner. The bed, which differs from the Egyptian model in that it has a headpiece as

(*right*) Stone relief from the Assyrian palace of Sennacherib, of about 700 BC, showing a high throne-like chair, with a footstool. Both have cone-shaped blocks at the ends of the feet

(*far right*) Stone relief from Persia, from the 6th century BC, depicting the lower part of a throne. Animal paws are incorporated in the centre of the leg sections

an integral part of the frame, is likewise raised high above the ground in a dominating position. One feature of Assyrian furniture not found in the Egyptian styles is the use of inverted cone-shaped blocks under the feet of chairs or beds.

The furniture of ancient Persia resembles in many respects the Assyrian forms, largely because the Persians took over the dominions of Assyria and Babylon and absorbed much of their art, culture and building techniques. In the ruins of the city of Persepolis, built by Darius the Great (c.520–c.486 BC), stone reliefs show the kind of furniture used by the royal family and its entourage. Again, the items are limited in variety, and thrones predominate. In the lower part of a Persian throne of this period, illustrated here, the animal paws are incorporated a little over half-way down the leg length. The turned legs with bulging contours appear to be a new, and not very attractive, feature of Persian design, but they mark the beginning of the technique of turning furniture members, a style that has continued ever since.

Greece and Rome

In the furniture of ancient Greece we encounter for the first time in the history of civilization more than one individual 'period' of furniture styles. The earlier pieces of the sixth century BC, in the time of oligarchic rule, were rigid and square, and appear to be directly in line with styles set by Egypt and Assyria. Perpendicular backs, square or turned straight legs occasionally terminating in animal hooves, and even straight arm-rests characterize the chairs. The beds and couches remain high, although they seem more luxuriously upholstered or cushioned than before.

From the fifth century BC the Greeks became more and more involved in wars with the Persian empire, which sought to dominate the Greek city states. They also began developing more democratic ideas of government. This struggle to maintain independence was accompanied by a great liberation of artistic genius, free from the influence of the Near East, which was embodied in architecture, sculpture, pottery and furniture.

The new Greek furniture represented a distinct breakaway

This relief of the 6th century BC illustrates the more rigid style of early Greek furniture

Greek *klismos* of the 5th century BC from a marble relief, now in the National Museum, Athens

from the rigidity of the past, and it was typified by graceful, flowing, curving lines which made the pieces relaxing in appearance and function. The most widely used articles were couches (now closer to the ground), tripod tables with animal legs, fixed and folding stools, and the *klismos,* or upright chair.

The *klismos* had a square seat on four sabre-shaped legs, and a curved back. The rear legs extended upwards on either side of the seat in the same arc to a cross member and then changed direction inwards to support a curved backboard. The four members of the seat were mortised into the legs, giving the legs a measure of elasticity which enabled the chair to be used comfortably on rough ground and which prevented it being tipped over backwards or forwards. The height of the backboard varied; if it was low the sitter could rest an arm on it. (This is well illustrated by a seated marble figure in the Capitoline Museum in Rome.) For more formal occasions the higher back variety was always available.

While our knowledge of Greek furniture is restricted to descriptions in literature and portrayal in sculpture, reliefs and pottery, many pieces of Roman furniture have survived, even though they are in marble, stone or bronze, or have bronze parts. A considerable quantity of pieces was found in the ruins of Herculaneum and Pompeii, which were excavated in the middle of the eighteenth century. It is clear that the marble and bronze pieces were modelled on earlier or con-

Stone relief of Roman basket-work armchair, of about the 3rd century AD

temporary articles made of wood. The objects were seldom original in style, and were imitations of earlier Greek forms. If anything, they were more relaxed in shape, like the couch of wood and bronze dating from the first century AD, or the stone relief of the basket-work chair of the third century AD, which may well have been one of the few Roman inventions.

Roman carpenters and furniture-makers developed a high standard of workmanship. They had at their disposal a variety of rare and attractive woods, such as satinwood, citruswood, olivewood, oak and cedarwood, to mention but a few. They excelled in inlay and veneer-work, using not only these woods which they had learned to colour by means of special dyes, but also ivory, ebony, gold and silver, and even tortoiseshell.

Their wood-carving of chairs and table legs, arm-rests, friezes, cornices, etc., was of the highest order of delicacy and sophistication, and this skill was certainly equalled by the makers of bronze and stone furniture. But despite the quality, the variety was restricted to a small range of articles, for the Roman taste in furniture was a simple one, confined largely to utilitarian pieces. The austerity of the Roman character of republican times was still evident in the heyday of the empire.

The couch, of course, was one of the principal pieces of furniture, for the Roman upper and middle classes, relieved of the burdens of work by a slave class, spent a great deal of their time at prolonged banquets, parties and discussions at which it was customary to recline on well-cushioned couches.

Roman bronze couch dating from the 1st century BC to 1st century AD, with wooden parts restored. It was found at Boscoreale

THE MIDDLE AGES

For centuries after the collapse of the Western Roman Empire in the fifth century AD there is no clear picture of the development of individual domestic furniture styles in Western Europe. Byzantium was now the capital of the Eastern Empire and of the Christian Church, and such pieces as can be dated and attributed to Western Europe were influenced by Byzantine furniture styles. In many cases they may have been made by Byzantine craftsmen. Among these are a sixth-century bishop's throne of ivory at Ravenna in Italy and a bronze throne supposedly made in about 600 AD and used by the Frankish king Dagobert I (628–639). The latter is based on the folding stool principle of construction.

In the Eastern Roman Empire, meanwhile, the craft of

(right) Ivory throne for a bishop, made at Ravenna in the 6th century AD. Its shape and carving are strongly Byzantine

(far right) Italian chest of the 8th century, displaying clearly the influence of Byzantium. The metal band is small for the size of chest and may not be original

furniture-making continued unabated, although its styles became more and more ecclesiastical. At the same time these styles also reflected the older traditions of the Near East. The graceful and relaxed contours of classical Greece and Rome gave way to upright, rigid and uncomfortable lines like the Ravenna ivory throne, which itself was closer to ancient Persian thrones. But if the gracefulness diminished, the carving and the embellishment retained their high quality, in some cases bearing comparison with the best Roman work. And when the secret of silk manufacture, for centuries the monopoly of China, was revealed in the middle of the sixth century by two Byzantine monks who had smuggled some silk-worm eggs back to Greece from the East, silk-weaving leapt into importance as an industry, not least for the drapery and upholstery of furniture.

When furniture-making as a skill reappears in Western Europe the earliest pieces of any merit are ecclesiastical, and for the most part they are fixed items, such as stalls, prayer benches, etc., in early churches. Gradually, more attention was paid to movable articles like stools and chests. Folding stools were as popular as they had been in earlier days, and

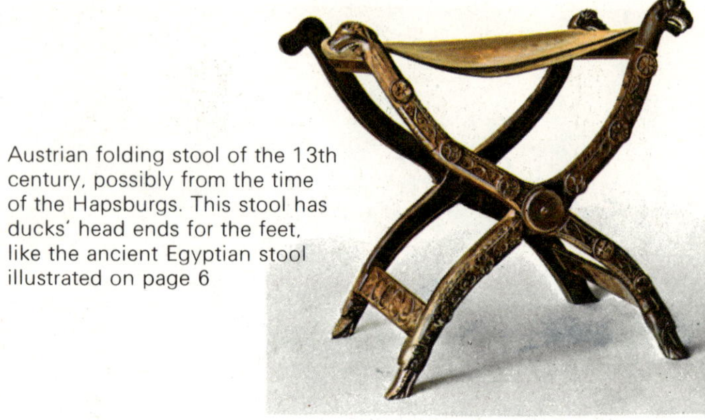

Austrian folding stool of the 13th century, possibly from the time of the Hapsburgs. This stool has ducks' head ends for the feet, like the ancient Egyptian stool illustrated on page 6

now they took two distinct forms: one for ecclesiastical use and the other for regal or military use. It was the chest, however, that appears to have received the greatest attention.

When a feudal system of land ownership began to evolve in Western Europe in the sixth and seventh centuries, landlords began to accumulate domestic possessions, such as clothing, jewellery and household utensils. The nature of their way of life – they had to travel incessantly about their often extensive territories – involved continual cartage of their belongings. Not only did seats and beds have to be easily dismantled and then reassembled, but a variety of smaller pieces of equipment also had to be transported because they were in constant use. For this, the wooden chest became indispensable.

For centuries, then, an enormous variety of sizes and shapes of chest was produced in nearly every country in Western Europe, for both secular and ecclesiastical use. Many of them were embellished with fine carving. Some were bound with decorative ironwork strips, and even the earliest ones had iron locks or clasps. Tops were flat or gabled; if flat they would be used as seats when they were not being transported, and eventually they were made to stand on legs which were extensions of the vertical end members.

Not long after the Norman invasions of Italy and England in the eleventh century the first cupboards since Roman times appear in Europe. They are crudely constructed, in some cases so much so that they are painted with portraits or figures in vivid colours to hide the indifferent workmanship at the joints.

The same crude and uneven quality pervades surviving chairs, benches and couches from these centuries, and the best craftsmanship is confined to woodwork in ecclesiastical buildings, such as the great cathedrals and abbeys which were springing up from Wales to Austria and from Scotland to Spain in the eleventh, twelfth, thirteenth and fourteenth centuries.

The fifteenth century marked the introduction of new styles of furniture-making in Europe. Loosely described by later generations as Gothic, like the architecture of the same name, they embodied decorative motifs such as tracery, finials, pointed arches and foliage. The quality of construction also improved. Chests, for example, ceased to be just assemblages of thick planks, with here and there exuberant but not very delicate carving. They began to be made of wood in a proper framework, with rails, thin panelling and architectural ornament. They also assumed proper proportions.

The changes were first seen in Flanders where some of the towns had become extremely prosperous by virtue of the cloth trade or through shipping. One new piece of furniture which appeared was the *dressoir,* a tall structure consisting of a chest with doors, supported by a stand on a plinth, a natural development from the chest. The gap between the chest part and the plinth could be used for displaying exceptional items of metalware or pottery. The chest part was more or less at eye level, and therefore suitable for storage of cups, small ewers, etc.

Chests were also developed into settles with backs and sides. The area beneath the main box part began to be utilized for drawers. A whole new vista of ornamentation opened, in which asymmetry was a distinguishing feature. This is clear from the carving on the front of the chest from France illustrated here. One popular type of wood ornament was linenfold, and some of the best examples of this type of carving came from England. Much of the tracery was of ecclesiastical origin, imitating as it did the beautiful creative work in stone and wood from the cathedrals and abbeys, and this is easy to

(*left*) Detail of Perpendicular tracery from a similar chest

(*below*) Late 15th-century Gothic chest from France, with Perpendicular tracery and asymmetrical foliage

understand in an age when religion played a dominant part in all men's lives.

The principal feature, however, of this Gothic period of furniture was the appearance, for the first time, of furniture fashions. Different regions of Western Europe enjoyed individual vogues of design and manufacture. In fifteenth-century France, for example, the ornamentation on wood concentrated on foliage and animal designs and it was generally very elaborate. This was made easier by the increasing use of walnut, a wood that is softer than the oak which continued to predominate in England and Germany.

When the influence of the Italian Renaissance first made itself felt in Western Europe it began by superficial decorative impositions on basic Gothic styles. But the acceptance of the new philosophical ideas of the Renaissance among thinking people led to Renaissance furniture styles superseding altogether the Gothic-ecclesiastical style. Resistance to this change lasted longest in England.

A good example of a Gothic style *dressoir*, from France in the 15th century. There is a small drawer under the cupboard doors in the top part

THE RENAISSANCE

Italy

The Renaissance, a term that has never been satisfactorily defined, began in Italy somewhere about the end of the fourteenth century. It means, roughly, the revival in Europe of Greek and Roman ideals in art, literature and architecture, and it marks the beginning of the end of the Middle Ages. Gradually, however, the Renaissance replaced the Gothic taste.

This return to the ideas of ancient Greece and Rome extended to furniture, but in so doing limitations were at once placed upon design, because few genuine relics of classical furniture had survived. What was learned came from literature or from sculpture and stone reliefs. Furniture-makers in fact took existing patterns, not only of ancient Greece and Rome but also of Gothic styles, and tried to improve upon them by making them conform to the principles of classical architecture, particularly with larger pieces of furniture. To a great extent they succeeded, but many early Renaissance pieces remained crude in their proportions, especially when compared with the buildings of the Italian architects of the time.

There were some notable exceptions, however, particularly the di Giovanni cupboard which, made in about 1500, is now at the Abbazia di Monte Oliveto Maggiore, near Siena. This splendid piece not only demonstrates the best in Italian Renaissance furniture design according to architectural principles. It is also an excellent example of the art of intarsia. This technique began in Italy in Byzantine times and reached great heights in Florence in the late fifteenth century, where its greatest exponent was Francesco di Giovanni.

Intarsia is a form of wood marquetry which is made up of polygonal tesserae of wood, bone, mother-of-pearl and metal in geometric patterns. To accentuate differences in colour and shade the woods used were dyed or scorched. A development of the art was pictorial intarsia, and the *trompe-l'œil*

This Italian Renaissance interior has a fine chimneypiece with heraldic decoration. Some of the furniture has characteristics of earlier styles, such as Gothic

form was a remarkable version. It produced a three-dimensional picture by virtue of creating an optical illusion. The illustrated panel is an excellent example.

Italian furniture-makers improved upon a number of traditional pieces. The folding stool, for centuries limited to a seat supported by two pairs of crossed members articulating at the centre of the X, now had a row of crossed leg members close together, and the legs extended upwards beyond the seat in graceful curves. Chests, coffers and box seats were also very greatly improved. A chest now became a single unit with an architectural decoration of cornice and plinth, and sometimes pilasters. They were made chiefly of walnut which when stained and varnished took on a soft

(*right*) Italian walnut folding stool, of the early 16th century, which has a back as well as arms. The back was detachable. These stools are sometimes called X-shaped stools

(*left*) Intarsia panel with perspective decoration in various woods. Late 15th century, from Urbino

(*right*) This early Italian Renaissance box settle has clear architectural features

dark brown hue that accentuated the architectural profile.

Dining tables of the period generally had rectangular tops supported at each end by strong consoles, connected by a stretcher. The feet of the consoles sometimes took the form of lions' paws, like classical Roman marble tripod tables, and in fact a great deal of trouble was taken in decorating these consoles, which even included boldly sculptured grotesques.

New pieces of the period included writing desks which had drawers on either side of a central niche for the knees. Chairs remained essentially upright, often with straight square legs, and much attention was paid to both carving and upholstery. Velvet cushions, velvet or leather seat coverings for stuffed seats, fixed with large-bossed nails, made the chairs more comfortable than their predecessors, but there was still no return to the relaxed sabre-leg chair style of ancient Greece and Rome, presumably because no examples were found.

The furniture styles of the Italian Renaissance spread to all Western Europe, gradually merging with, or superseding, the Gothic styles. The concentration on architectural principles, and the new boldness and diversity of the forms of carving, painting and gilding of furniture, prepared the ground for a whole range of locally varying styles in Europe. Each of the main countries was to have its own particular Renaissance, in furniture as well as in the other arts, and it is interesting to see national styles growing out of this great movement.

Germany

The Italian Renaissance influenced the art, architecture and furniture of southern Germany far more swiftly than it did Germany north of the river Main. The principal centre of art was Nuremberg and there, under the lead of the great craftsman Peter Flötner (d. 1546), Renaissance ornamental forms were 'transplanted' onto German chests, cupboards, box seats, *dressoirs* and other pieces. Flötner's influence was decisive on German furniture, and before his death in the middle of the sixteenth century the new styles had spread throughout southern Germany, crossed into the north and even reached Flanders.

Flötner was a designer who produced a series of woodcuts that provided patterns for carvers and furniture-makers. One large cupboard, made of oak and ash to his design in about 1540 at Nuremberg, clearly demonstrates the grasp he had of Italian Renaissance ideas. It is typical of the new shape of cupboards, although it had four small doors and not two

Mid 16th-century canopy bed from North Germany. The carved figures in the panels above the bed base are from the Bible

Large oak and ash cupboard made from a design by Peter Flötner *c.* 1540 at Nuremberg. A fine example of German Renaissance furniture

large ones. Between the upper and lower sections is an intermediate section with two drawers, and this scheme is repeated in the plinth assembly below the lower half. The top is ornamented with a frieze and dentil cornice.

After Flötner German pieces adopted more and more of the Italian styles and the architectural elements became more pronounced. A writing desk made in about 1554 has a front which looks like the façade of a Renaissance cathedral or grand house, with Corinthian columns supporting pediments, and with highly decorative panelling. The fact that it is a desk seems to be an afterthought, for the sloping table top starts midway down behind the façade. German furniture-makers also began to specialize in inlay-work, using boxwood, ebony, ivory, metal and even marble inserts. This had an interesting result. Their descendants played an important part in the

Dutch 17th-century interior showing typical furniture of the period, including a draw-top refectory table and plain leather-upholstered chairs. Panelling was a common feature in the houses of prosperous Dutch merchants

splendid marquetry productions of the Louis XV and Louis XVI periods of French furniture.

In the northern part of Germany the Renaissance styles were assimilated more slowly. Gothic-style chests and cupboards, for example, continued to be made well into the sixteenth century, and the cruder form of construction of solid oak boarding persisted. But even if the Gothic styles endured, the wood-carving already reflects Renaissance ideas, that is, panels depicting Biblical, religious or classical scenes. In the middle of the sixteenth century northern German furniture began also to absorb the ideas of Flemish Renaissance designs (see page 27), especially those of Floris and his school at Antwerp. Furniture framework was often decorated with caryatids and hermae. Before long, the intarsia work of Italy reached northern Germany where it enjoyed great popularity.

The Low Countries

Some of the best Gothic furniture had come out of the rich towns in Flanders, such as Brussels, Liège and Antwerp, and it was in these places that the new styles of the Italian Renaissance took root. Flemish furniture of the later fifteenth century already shows the influence of architectural principles, and in the first half of the next century Flemish styles reached a high standard of Renaissance form under Cornelis Bos and Cornelis Floris, the latter a carver of quite exceptional skill who specialized in grotesques and scroll-work.

Perhaps the leading influence, however, was Hans Vredeman de Vries of Antwerp, painter, architect and engineer, who published a variety of furniture designs. Some were in a book called *Differents Pourctraites de Menuiserie,* and this book had a profound influence on furniture in the Low Countries generally. Although the furniture had already adopted the

Renaissance 'look', de Vries and his followers made Low Countries furniture among the finest outside Italy. De Vries' son, Paul, continued his father's important work, publishing further volumes of designs in 1630. Cupboards, tables, chairs, beds, chests were ornamented in the best Renaissance tradition with a variety of new motifs. One of de Vries' designs was for a long refectory table with the Flemish-style draw-top. Two sections of the same thickness and which together make up the same length as the top are drawn out and raised to the same level as the top to make a very long table. The framework is supported by legs which are balusters with cubes, etc., linked by stretchers at the lower end and resting on bun feet. Carving was an important mode of decoration on the heavy wooden cabinets and chests so popular with the wealthy Dutch burghers. Biblical and classical scenes, geometrical shapes and Renaissance floral motifs overwhelm the surface of these cupboards. Dutch interiors were usually panelled in rich woods and the carved furniture was especially designed to fit in with this fashion.

Early 17th-century Dutch draw-top refectory table of oak with ebony inlaid panels, after a design by Vredeman de Vries of Antwerp

Dutch ebony chair of the early 17th century, with carved leatherwork, showing rigidity of construction

Chairs remained upright and fairly rigid, though leather seats and backs became fashionable. The leather was elaborately carved, like Spanish chair backs, and the tops of the two vertical chair back members were often headed by carved animal faces, which were sometimes gilded.

Low Countries furniture, especially that of the United Provinces, later called Holland, was to change again. The expansion of Dutch interests in the East and the prosperity this brought Holland was the cause in the seventeenth century of the development of individual furniture styles employing a variety of new, rare and exciting woods.

France

The last years of the fifteenth and the first part of the sixteenth century were years of national glory for France. Her armies invaded and conquered parts of Italy, and thus brought France directly into contact with the splendours of the Renaissance, which was then at its height. Francis I (1515–1547) tried several times to extend French territory in Italy, but was invariably thwarted in the end. Gradually, his appreciation of art outweighed the attraction of military campaigns, and he began to encourage Italian artists and craftsmen to come and work in France, especially for his court at Paris. He employed the artists Rosso and Primaticcio at Fontainebleau, where they consolidated the hold the Renaissance had already taken on French art and architecture.

But while the merger of Gothic and Renaissance styles proved so successful in Paris, and at other towns in the centre and south, partly because of the increase in the use of walnut wood, which was easier to carve and more attractively grained than woods used earlier, older and starker Gothic styles persisted in the north where there was an almost stubborn adherence to oak.

Outside Italy, Renaissance French furniture was among the best in Europe. Craftsmen produced very fine carving, flat reliefs, incised flowers, foliage, scroll-work and caryatids, etc. In the 1550s the architect Androuet Ducerceau published pattern books of furniture design, and these exerted a strong influence on French styles. Particular emphasis was laid on cabinets, and in those times one of the most popular woods for cabinets was ebony – hard, black and expensive. Only the rich could afford pieces of ebony furniture, and so arose a select group of craftsmen called *ébénistes,* a term which later came to mean makers of cabinet-type furniture as opposed to *menuisiers* who made solid wood articles such as chairs. Furniture-makers of the French Renaissance produced fine pieces, but as yet their work did not reveal the incomparable skill and gracefulness that was to mark the furniture of their descendants in the eighteenth century.

Design for French Renaissance canopy bed, of the late 16th century, by the architect Ducerceau

Spain and Portugal

Spain was not a united nation until the very end of the fifteenth century, when the vigorous, gallant and cultivated Moors were expelled by Ferdinand V of Aragon. At first, therefore, only northern Spanish furniture was influenced by the Italian Renaissance, and the southern styles remained distinctly Oriental. Indeed, although the Moors left Spain, the Oriental ideas which they had brought with them had become an integral part of Spanish life, and from the sixteenth century onwards whatever styles were dominant, there was always something of the East to be detected in the designs.

One piece peculiar to Spanish furniture was the *vargueño,* or writing cabinet. This was a box with a flap front which was let down to horizontal level for writing. The box stood on a special stand, two parallel horizontal supports of which, immediately under box level, drew out to hold the flap steady. The flap was heavily decorated either in metalwork banding, escutcheons, etc., or inlaid with ivory, boxwood and other materials, often in patterns strongly suggestive of Oriental origin.

The interior of the *vargueño* was a complex of drawers, rectangular or square, together with one or two cupboards, in varying sizes, also inlaid with Moorish or Renaissance motifs. Renaissance influence was particularly apparent in the incorporation of architectural features, such as columns and pediments. The wood for the carcase and main members was usually walnut. Later cabinets acquired two doors hung vertically instead of a flap and stood on bun feet. In this form they were usually larger than the *vargueño* and were used for storage. In another form there were two halves in one piece, a *vargueño*-type structure with falling flap on the top and a two- or four-doored cabinet below, forerunners of the eighteenth-century writing cabinets, or *secrétaires à abattant*.

Spanish chairs, like nearly all contemporary ones in Europe, retained their upright and rigid style, but wide use was made of leather back panels between the two upright back

Walnut *vargueños* of the late 16th century were a typical Spanish item of Renaissance furniture. This example, which is shown both open and closed, has architectural features on the drawer fronts and small cupboard doors (*left*)

Spanish Renaissance pine cupboard with simple architectural features and geometrical mouldings on the panels (*right*)

supports. Velvet upholstery was popular, and was enriched by ornamental brass studding and gold fringe or braid. Cupboards assumed architectural proportions and were often finely carved, even if sometimes more simply than in other countries.

Portugal, which had been an independent kingdom since the twelfth century, also produced fine furniture in similar styles. After the discovery of the route to India via the Cape by Vasco da Gama (1497–1499) and the consequent opening up of trading posts in the East, Portuguese furniture displayed marked Oriental influences especially in the inlay-work. Some pieces were made of a red-brown wood which served to accentuate the effect of the inlay-work.

This oak inlaid writing desk of about 1590 illustrates how primitive English marquetry-work was in the 16th century. The desk is in the Victoria and Albert Museum

England

The Middle Ages to the Restoration

English furniture of the Middle Ages had little to recommend it either in style or in excellence of craftsmanship. Linenfold carving (see page 17) was one of a few exceptions. England was also slow to accept the new Renaissance styles, especially in outlying parts of the country where the craftsmen were – and continued to be right into the nineteenth century – extraordinarily conservative. The early inlay-work was poor compared with contemporary German, French or Italian work. When Renaissance ornamentation did appear in England it was considerably more restrained than examples from the rest of Europe and the architectural designs seem to have been definitely 'watered down'.

Despite the inferior quality of English inlay-work, it was used on a fairly wide scale, not only on pieces made for the rich but also on more simple furniture in humble homes. Many pieces made in both the sixteenth and seventeenth centuries were decorated with wood inlay of box, holly-wood and 'bog oak' (which had a very dark tinge). Patterns varied considerably, but there was a noticeable preference for geometric designs, known as parquetry, and for squares and lozenges. The writing box illustrates both the poor quality of the work and the preference for parquetry.

This inferior standard was to improve very greatly in the middle of the seventeenth century and in the Restoration period marquetry was being done in England that compared well with European standards.

In the time of Elizabeth I the heightening of national pride and the growing wealth of the new middle classes provided opportunities for bolder experiment among craftsmen. Italian styles became popular, not least for upholstered furniture, such as sofas and chairs. While some pieces in great

Beechwood upholstered couch. This English piece follows the Renaissance style and is bolder than most contemporary English furniture

houses show considerable experimentation there seems to have been an undercurrent of simplicity in furniture which became more emphasized as the nation, for the most part, began to lean towards the Puritan ideal of life. Tables and chairs, especially, retained a severity of style that was not present in other countries. Armchairs with rush seats and high backs of three or four cross-bars (wrongly called ladder-back chairs) were simple and staid, and fitted in well with the new austerity.

Most furniture in England of the period was made of oak, although country pieces were occasionally made of one or other kind of fruitwood. Walnut was used for veneering, although not on the same scale as in Europe. But as the taste for walnut, with its superior grain for veneer and with its suitability for solid construction, increased in popularity, walnut trees began to be planted in England. It was expected that in half a century a rich harvest would become available for furniture-making. Such a harvest was not forthcoming. Although many trees were planted and quantities of walnut thus made available, much of it was of poor quality. Conse-

Typical English 17th-century oak gate-legged table. It is functional rather than aesthetic, but the style was nonetheless copied thousands of times over

The English produced some very fine oak refectory tables in the earlier half of the 17th century. This example is in the Victoria and Albert Museum

quently, the better walnuts used in Europe for furniture had to be imported.

Typical of the items that have survived from Tudor and early Stuart times are settles with box seats, both the movable kind and the kind that fits a window recess, the table bench with a back which slides up and across to make a table top, gate-legged tables with two hinged flaps and a gate on each of the longer sides of the central rectangular top, and a continued variety of chests, boxes and coffers used both as seats and for storage. These chests were properly constructed with thin wood panelling between the main members, carved either simply or elaborately.

One piece of considerable importance in the larger houses was the bed. A number of late Tudor and early Stuart examples have survived and they reflect the progress of English furniture design. The bed has four posts supporting a canopy. The carving on the bed posts varies considerably, so does the width of the posts where they are turned. Sometimes the bulbs are narrowed so much as to be almost cut in half and they are quite out of proportion with the rest of the bed which usually has a break-front cornice at the top of the canopy with a vague claim to architectural style. In Stuart times the bulbing becomes generally narrower and so more attractive.

The Great Bed of Ware

But even if much of the furniture of the late sixteenth and early seventeenth century in England is not as ornate or as exuberant as that of its contemporaries in Europe, it was now so well made – and in such quantity – that a great deal of it has lasted to the present day. (The author was able, ten years ago, to purchase a Jacobean armchair with carved panel back and hexagonal legs for a trifling sum at a north-country auction.) Members were assembled by mortise and tenon, held by dowels, and sometimes glued as well. Pieces were not gilded in England as frequently as elsewhere, but were waxed and polished vigorously and often to produce a rich patina.

It seems that even as early as the sixteenth century wood-workers were experimenting with polishes which have hardly altered to this day. Boiled linseed oil rubbed into wood in its natural state accentuated the grain. Cabinetmakers today still advise using this treatment. Alternatively, they recommend turpentine and beeswax mixed, and this was probably being used in late Plantagenet times. No amount of modern silicon wax polishing will produce anything like the surface that these centuries-old recipes invariably do. French polishing is to be avoided at all costs.

English furniture does not really begin to bear comparison with European styles until the Restoration of Charles II in 1660, when rich exiles, who during their years abroad had familiarized themselves with the trends in European art and craftsmanship, came home to commission work for the houses they were to build or rebuild in a new age that was liberal not only in the field of art.

17th-century oak chairs in England were for a long time severe and rigid in style, but they were also well made. This oak chair with elaborately carved back was made in about 1650

THE SEVENTEENTH AND EIGHTEENTH CENTURIES

France

Henry IV, Louis XIII and Louis XIV

French furniture of the seventeenth century falls roughly into two main periods. The earlier, covering the reigns of Henry IV, Louis XIII and the first years of Louis XIV, was heavily influenced by the styles of the late Italian Renaissance. The later period, during which Louis XIV invited all manner of artists and craftsmen to come and work in France, established itself as one of the supreme eras of furniture-making and was to have a vital influence on furniture design all over Europe.

In the earlier period Italian styles prevailed while Marie de Médicis (1573–1642), the Florentine wife, and later widow, of Henry IV dominated society, and after her death, when the Italian-born Cardinal Mazarin ruled France during the minority of Louis XIV. Under her patronage Italian craftsmen left Italy and flocked to Paris. They brought with them the fine skills of marquetry and intarsia, and gradually French furniture became less formal and rigid and less elaborate in carved ornamentation. More attention was paid to the

(*left*) Small Louis XIII table
(*right*) Early Louis XIV armchair with arm supports carved with acanthus leaves

upholstery of chairs, and special fabrics were created. Made chiefly of wool and called moquettes, the fabrics had intricate and multi-coloured patterns. Seats were over-stuffed and covered, bordered round the edges with brass studs or gold braid, and chair backs became more comfortable with improved upholstering. The more solid furniture, such as gate-legged tables and *armoires,* surrendered much of their earlier carving, and legs and pilasters were turned or twisted like sticks of barley sugar.

Mazarin died in 1661 and Louis XIV, now twenty-three, assumed control of his own kingdom. He inherited a secure throne, a full treasury, a people filled with national pride, and a country in which brigandage had been put down and it was now safe to travel without having to regard one's home as a fortress. Then began a golden age for France.

Louis set out to make Paris the intellectual and artistic centre of Europe. He appointed Jean Baptiste Colbert (1619–1683) one of Mazarin's most able assistants, as controller-general of finances, with instructions, among other things, to ensure that there was enough money to attract to Paris the best available artists and craftsmen. Louis and Colbert set up a state organization called *La Manufacture Royale des Meubles de la Couronne,* with premises on the city outskirts at Gobelins. At its head they put Charles Le Brun, one of the leading artists of the day. He was appointed royal director of art and was commissioned to supervise the construction and adornment of the new palace the king proposed to build around an old hunting lodge at Versailles which his father had used. The decorations, furnishings, paintings, etc., were to be made in the Gobelins factory.

Le Brun personally supervised the work of this great organization, for which he provided the bulk of the designs, and for a generation nothing emerged that did not carry the mark of his genius. The workshop acquired the highest reputation, and the craftsmen there were better paid than anywhere in Europe. French workers moreover mixed well with the large number of foreign craftsmen. When he died in 1690 Le Brun was followed by Jean Bérain (1638–1711), a great artist who may be said to have heralded the coming of the Rococo style (see page 52). By that time *ébénistes, menuisiers* and bronze-makers had started to branch out on their own and issue their own designs and products. There were the *fondeurs-ciseleurs*, who cast and roughly chased the bronzes, and the *ciseleurs-doreurs,* who finely chased and gilded them. Not all bronzes were gilded. There were two guilds of the latter operating at this time.

The principal pieces of Louis XIV furniture of this time were cupboards, chests, cabinets on stands, medallion cabinets, low cupboards with marquetry panelling, bureaux, glazed cupboards, consoles and day-beds. Cabinet pieces were enriched either by the new tortoiseshell and brass inlay-work, made popular in France by André-Charles Boulle (1642–1732), or by multi-coloured wood marquetry of laburnum, holly, sycamore, pearwood, etc., which had begun in Italy and which was to be developed by French craftsmen to a degree unmatched in the history of furniture. Solid pieces, such as chairs, beds, etc., were often gilded, silvered or painted. Some pieces were actually made for Louis XIV entirely of silver.

Boulle marquetry became very popular for a long time, and to some extent it predominated in the decoration of cabinet furniture for the rest of Louis XIV's reign. It was copied widely not only in France but also abroad, especially in Germany. Boulle himself had workshops in the Louvre, a great privilege, in which four sons were trained and then served as assistants. It became a thriving business, and before long they were also making pieces of furniture with wood marquetry. Boulle tortoiseshell and metal inlay was confined to cabinets, cupboards, large and small, and other pieces which were mainly rectilinear.

In the nineteenth century a considerable quantity of this type of furniture was made in Europe along eighteenth-century French lines. It was often called Buhl, perhaps the nearest German equivalent to Boulle, but sometimes it was a very poor imitation of the original. There is still a great deal of this Buhl furniture about, some of it admittedly fine, masquerading even in reputable salerooms as eighteenth-century tortoiseshell and metal inlay 'in the manner of A. C. Boulle'.

At the end of the seventeenth century the influence of Jean Bérain spread to furniture design. He produced a variety of patterns for craftsmen in which architectural forms became

An excellent example of the tortoiseshell and brass marquetry-work of A.-C. Boulle (1642–1732)

less important and pieces acquired the look of sculpture. It was in fact a sort of transition from Baroque to Rococo. At this time the cabriole leg began to replace the square or turned leg and it dominated furniture legs for more than sixty years in France, although the other forms reappeared from time to time (see Louis XVI furniture).

Two pieces of furniture were becoming fashionable, the bureau and the chest of drawers, the latter known in France as the commode. Two main kinds of bureau were made: a writing table with drawers and long curving, or occasionally straight, legs, and a table which had drawers below the table top, on both sides of a centre kneehole. This type of desk is sometimes called a pedestal desk in England. At first these pieces were supported by eight legs, but as the freer spirit of Bérain's ideas spread, four legs were considered more aesthetic.

The first decade of the eighteenth century was marked, so far as France was concerned, by a most expensive war with Britain, Holland and Austria. A succession of very able French marshals were severely beaten in battle by the incomparable Marlborough. Although the end result of the war was perhaps not so disastrous to French military prestige as was once thought, the campaign emptied the national treasury, and it effectively put an end to the golden age of Louis XIV. Much of the gold and silver plating and ornamentation at Versailles and other royal buildings, which had been produced in Le Brun's time, had to be melted down to provide hard cash, including all of Louis' solid silver pieces. As a result we have never been able to appreciate the exquisite beauty of this type of work.

For some years following the defeat of the French armies French furniture-makers lacked the encouragement they had enjoyed in earlier times. Some of the craftsmen began to look to the king's nephew, Philip, Duke of Orleans, for patronage. He was to become Regent for the child-king, Louis XIV's great grandson. Thus began the period known as the Régence.

(*top*) Pedestal table with fine Boulle marquetry panelling, after a design by Bérain and dating from 1690 to 1700, (*centre*) Louis XIV day-bed in giltwood with elaborately carved stretchers, (*bottom*) Commode, veneered in kingwood, from the end of the 17th century

The Régence

French furniture reached the zenith of achievement in the eighteenth century. The styles, and the craftsmanship with which individual pieces were made, were unquestionably the finest in the history of furniture.

The styles fall into four main periods, Régence (c.1710–c.1735), Louis XV (c.1735–c.1760), Transitional (c.1760–c.1770) and Louis XVI (c.1770–c.1795). There was a fifth period, the Directoire (c.1795–c.1805), but this is not comparable with the other four.

Régence furniture was lighter and gayer than that of Louis XIV; Boulle marquetry gave way to wood marquetry, and the Rococo style, with its asymmetry, superseded the heavy cornice and panel decoration of the Baroque. The influence of

Régence gilt console of about 1725, from a design by Oppenord. It is a fine example of Rococo gilt woodwork

This very handsome *bureau-plat* was made by Cressent in about 1730. It is in kingwood and tulipwood veneer. The mounts were probably made by Cressent as well

Bérain was predominant for a long time. Historically, the Régence lasted but eight years, 1715–1723, but the new styles of furniture began before 1715 and carried on well into the fourth decade of the century. We see the introduction of fantastic designs in bronze mounts, based on shell and rock forms, with elaborate flowers and foliage, curves and scroll-work, which overran the wood frames.

We have seen that the *ébénistes* had become independent craftsmen, even if employed by the Crown, and some of them like Boulle and Charles Cressent were making very prosperous livings out of their businesses. Their work was individual although it subscribed to certain fundamental principles. They were catering for an aristocracy which enjoyed considerable wealth and the leisure that came with it. Thus the furniture was both practical and comfortable. The legs of chairs and sofas, for example, became shorter, chair backs were lower, chair arms were placed further back on the seat and not directly over the front legs. It has been said that the changes in women's dress fashions led to this widening and deepening of chairs, or that the lowering of the height of men's wigs, which allowed a lower chair back, was responsible. In fact it is more likely to have been for architectural reasons.

The Regent, who was the nephew of Louis XIV, lived at the

Palais Royal in Paris, which had once been owned by Cardinal Richelieu. He also had a country house at Bagnolet. In each of these two residences an architect presided over the work of improving the decoration and furnishing. In Paris it was Gilles-Marie Oppenord and at Bagnolet a man of very different taste, Christophe Huet, who was a disciple of Bérain. The principal furniture-maker for both places was Cressent (1685–1768).

Although Cressent was by no means the only *ébéniste* of the time – we have evidence of over thirty *ébénistes* and *menuisiers* working in the period – catalogues of his works have survived, as have accounts of his dealings with the Crown, and we can in the absence of such evidence for other people regard him as the most representative of his time.

Since each piece of furniture made personally by Cressent took many months to complete there cannot have been many in his total output during the Régence period. What is more, Cressent very rarely signed his furniture, since in those days it had neither become compulsory to stamp pieces with makers' names nor was it even customary. Thus only a few can definitely be ascribed to Cressent. They are particularly fine, as the illustrations show, and his liberal use of bronze mounts in the wonderful Rococo style set an example to many *ébénistes* who were to follow.

During the Régence France managed to revive its trading activities after a period of recession following the costly War of the Spanish Succession. Considerable business was done in the West Indies where several islands had already become French possessions, and one result was the introduction of new woods such as mahogany, satinwood, rosewood (often known as kingwood), and purplewood. These became fashionable for marquetry-work when the popularity of Boulle tortoiseshell and metalwork waned.

For some time there had been two guilds of *fondeurs*-

(*right*) Purplewood clock and cabinet by Cressent, about 1740

(*left*) Another fine example of Cressent's work, a Régence commode of matched kingwood veneer, heavily decorated in bronze. It is probably based upon a design by Pineau

ciseleurs and *ciseleurs-doreurs,* who tried to monopolize bronze mount making, but many *ébénistes* made their own mounts. In the Louis XV period the guilds became strong enough to insist on being given this work. Cressent was prosecuted by the guilds on several occasions for having the work done in his own workshops, and so were others.

The eighteenth century saw the growth of the number of smaller rooms with a special function in great houses such as rooms for sewing, writing, dressing, etc., and this dictated a need for small pieces of furniture. One of these was the *encoignure,* or corner cupboard, which had first been designed in the last years of Louis XIV's reign. It now became a regular item in the house. *Encoignures* were usually made in pairs, sometimes in the same style as a commode which would be placed between them. Other new pieces were *bonheurs-du-jour,* which were ladies' writing desks, and small writing tables.

The Rococo style in furniture was greatly enhanced by the ideas of Juste Aurèle Meissonnier, who was designer to the king from 1726. He published a profuse range of designs for decoration and furniture in the asymmetrical *rocaille* form. The shell, in a variety of modes, becomes an important

feature in both marquetry work and in solid furniture. Chair backs now exposed the wooden surround of the frame, whether upholstered or carved, and the shell took the central position. Chairs were often painted, gilded or silvered, and it was usual for the raw woodwork to be treated in one of these ways. Many surviving chairs of the period that are now in the plain wood state were once so decorated.

A word should be added of the continuing popularity of lacquered furniture, a style which developed in the seventeenth century. Lacquered cabinets made in the East, for example in China or Japan, were imported and put on home-made stands. At the turn of the century some *ébénistes* tried to imitate genuine lacquer-work, but with indifferent results. A better effect was obtained by importing the main front panelling and building it into an indigenous framework. In about 1730 Guillaume Martin and his brothers were granted permission, for twenty years, to market on a large scale a new transparent lac varnish mixed with colour which they had invented. This enabled *ébénistes* to produce lacquered furniture of a much higher quality than the imitators of the previous generation, and, mounted with fine bronze-work, lacquer pieces maintained popularity for many years.

The merging of Régence styles into Louis XV styles was a gradual process, but by 1735 to 1740 it is clear that a new era of furniture-making was on the way.

(*left*) This cane seat chair of about 1730 illustrates the use of *rocaille* decoration on furniture, following Meissonnier. It has not been gilded or painted

(*right*) Lacquered furniture in France was in great demand throughout the period. This *encoignure* incorporates a panel of Chinese lacquer and was made in about 1740

Louis XV

The Louis XV period marked the height of the Rococo influence in French furniture. The architectural approach surrendered to over-elaborate decoration in bubbling, flowing bronze-work and fantastic designs in marquetry. Bronze decoration was so ornate that it concealed rather than heightened the lines of the wood parts. A host of new pieces was devised, partly to satisfy the tastes of women whose influence in society was growing and partly to provide new shapes for *ébénistes* and bronze makers to decorate. The excessive use of bronze, moreover, meant that more could be charged for pieces of furniture, in an age when the court and the nobility were spending on an unprecedented scale. No heed seems to have been given to the rumblings beneath the surface, which clearly pointed to the storm that was to break in the next generation.

The taste for Rococo furniture, as we have seen, received much of its impetus from Meissonnier and his drawings. The best *ébénistes* made furniture to his designs, and even Jacques Caffieri, the foremost bronze maker, modelled mounts in the

This very graceful chaise longue in carved walnut and upholstered in damask, made in about 1760, typifies the comfort of Louis XV furniture styles

Early Louis XV *bureau-plat*, of about 1745, with tulipwood and kingwood veneer, stamped Migeon, and also J. Dubois who may have repaired it at some time

Meissonnier manner, and sometimes signed them. This impetus extended beyond the borders of France, and Rococo styles are seen all over Western Europe, and to a lesser degree in England. Before long, too, foreign craftsmen again began to come to Paris to set up in business, and by the end of the period it is said that the majority of *ébénistes* were men of foreign birth. Some were the greatest of all the craftsmen, such as Oeben, Roger Lacroix (R.V.L.C.) and Riesener. All the same the style and the quality remained entirely French.

Louis XV styles of furniture were more relaxed and perhaps more comfortable than Régence. Sofas and day-beds, increasingly fashionable pieces for an indolent and carefree aristocracy, had gracefully undulating lines with exquisitely carved supports and backs, and were upholstered in light-coloured silks or printed cottons. *Bergère* chairs, with soft upholstered sides and often a loose cushion, emerged in the 1720s and swiftly became accepted in the best houses. They were extremely comfortable. Stools occupied an important place in large reception rooms since if the king or his family called, it was regarded as an honour to be allowed to sit on a stool in their presence.

Among the pieces on which *ébénistes* lavished their skill

Mid 18th-century Louis XV commode of tulipwood and kingwood. The very fine marquetry is typical of the work of P. Roussel

and time were *bureaux-plats*, drop-leaf desks, upright secretaires and commodes, A *bureau-plat*, already known in Louis XIV and Régence days, now became an essential item in aristocratic houses. Although it was a simple piece of furniture, that is, a table on long legs with a flat top and three drawers beneath the top, it lent itself to much adornment in bronze-work. Not only did the legs, the drawer fronts and the top corners receive elaborate mounts, but the whole periphery of the top was edged with ormolu moulding, shaped and bevelled in the serpentine or rectilinear outlines of the desk. In the top itself a sheet of leather was impressed, and the edges of this were gilded by the use of special tools.

Possibly the best known piece of the period, though not always the finest made nor most intricately decorated, was the commode. This was a chest with three drawers, or two drawers, or two main with two smaller drawers above. The front was bow-shaped, sometimes referred to as *bombé* to denote a swelling effect, with marquetry, parquetry or lacquer decoration, and it was adorned with bronze escutcheons, drawer handles and corner mounts. In many examples the bronze-work is extraordinarily elaborate. The earlier commodes generally had short legs with bronze *sabots* to protect the feet. Later on, longer legs and shorter carcases appeared, usually with two rather than three drawers. The colour of the marble for the top varied according to the colouring of the marble mantelpiece and other fittings in the room but the shaping of it followed the peripheral lines of the carcase. The edging was straight- or concave-chamfered.

It is generally believed that the best commodes have no dividing strip between the upper and lower drawer (or between upper and middle, and middle and lower), and indeed as a feature of design this strip seems to have gone out of fashion in the 1740s, at least in Paris-made furniture. Instead, the

Bernard van Risenburgh made this delightful *bureau à pente* in tulipwood, kingwood and other woods, in about 1760

whole front appears as a single panel, and the bronze mounts are designed to emphasize this.

The *bureau-plat* was a large writing table designed for use by men. Women of the age of Louis XV, who had little to do all day but gossip about this or that scandal, began to chronicle every-day events in diaries and note-books. Some even had more serious pretensions to literature. The result was that women wanted desks for themselves. The *ébénistes* obliged, and a variety of small writing tables were designed, some of them with mechanical devices which permitted a whole section containing pens, ink and blotting sand to rise or fall at the touch of a finger. Very great care was expended on these pieces and some wonderful examples have survived.

One particular desk in vogue was the *bureau à pente*. This was small and compact, and stood on long curving legs. It had an in-sloping flap which came down horizontally to provide a writing surface. When the flap was closed up, the desk occupied little space. These desks, and their companions,

Louis XV walnut *fauteuil* of about 1745. It is supremely elegant and comfortable

the *bonheurs-du-jour*, and other writing tables, gave the *ébénistes* fresh opportunities for displaying their unique skill in marquetry. Sèvres porcelain plaques were also used for decoration, although this ornamentation was more popular in the years 1760 to 1780.

Upright chairs of the Louis XV period were perhaps the finest in all furniture history. They combined elegance, functionalism and comfort to an unparalleled degree, whether they were richly upholstered and ornately carved or gilded, or simply polished and plainly covered.

Towards the end of the period there was a reaction against the curvaceous Rococo extravagances, and straighter lines began once more to be essential features of design. Bronze-

Encoignure of the mid 18th century by J. Dubois. It varies from other pieces made at this time in its return to plainer architectural lines. To some extent it also heralds Louis XVI fashions

This Cressent cabinet of about 1750 is an example of this great *ébéniste's* readiness to adopt new styles

work became more restrained and whole panels of plain veneer began to compete with marquetry. It was a rebellion against Rococo, fanned by the recent discoveries at the two Roman towns of Herculaneum and Pompeii, reports and drawings of which had been startling all Europe. But Rococo enthusiasts were not easily discouraged, and for some years a struggle between Rococo and Neo-classicism persisted in furniture. A cabinet in violetwood by Cressent, by now an old man but always ready to meet the demands of new tastes, perhaps embodies this conflict between Rococo and Neo-classicism.

A word should be said about the furniture-makers' guild and the practice of stamping furniture, for it was in the Louis XV period that stamping became obligatory. To succeed at all in the craft, a furniture-maker had to belong to the *Corporation Des Menuisiers-Ebénistes*. This guild protected its members from outside competition and it encouraged them to apprentice their children, as soon as they were old enough, into the craft of furniture-making. Several of the finest *ébénistes* of earlier years, such as Delorme, Dubois, Roussel and Migeon, had sons working, who produced fine pieces a generation later.

The aim of a guild member was to obtain a master's certificate, or become maître. To do this he not only had to serve several years' apprenticeship, he also had to make at least one exceptionally good piece which was submitted to a panel of maîtres for consideration. Once elected maître, he could then employ assistants, who in time might become maîtres themselves. This was how the guild expanded; it also accounts for the considerable quantity of very fine furniture made in the eighteenth century in France. Sometimes, a maître died and his business was carried on by his widow. Occasionally, the widow married the senior assistant who became the new chief of the workshop. This happened in the case of Oeben, whose widow married Riesener.

In the late 1740s a new series of regulations affecting the *Corporation Des Menuisiers-Ebénistes* was introduced. One was that every maître should sign his products before they left the workshop. He had to have an iron bar with his name raised in relief, known as a *maindron*, and this was struck with a hammer on to the back, or the underside, or the upright corner, or underneath the marble surmount, of a piece. The mark was registered with the guild headquarters. If the piece was acceptable the guild then stamped the initials JME, that is, *Jurande des Menuisiers Ebénistes*. Of course, many pieces escaped such scrutiny. Moreover, furniture made directly for the Crown was exempt from these regulations, and since much of this furniture was perhaps the best being made at the time, the presence of a stamp alone does not necessarily mean that the piece is the best obtainable.

Transitional

The Transitional period of French furniture covered the years from 1760 to 1770. It began with the conflict between Rococo and Neo-classical styles, or the merging of the two, and it ended with the triumph of the restraint of the latter over the exuberance of the former. It was a short period, but a very rich one. Many of the finest pieces of furniture of the whole eighteenth century were made in this decade. This may best be illustrated by considering the work of Oeben, who died in 1763, and the early work of Riesener, his chief assistant, who became maître in 1768. Other leading craftsmen of the time, whose work is often as fine as that of Oeben and Riesener, were J.-F. Leleu, G. Jacob, G. Joubert, N. Petit and Roger Lacroix, who abbreviated the other name he was known by (Roger Vandercruse La Croix) to R.V.L.C.

Commode by P. Roussel in tulipwood and sycamore, of about 1770. The marquetry is an exquisite example of *trompe l'oeil*

Provincial Transitional kingwood commode of two drawers with dividing strip. The drawer handles are Louis XVI style

What sort of changes did Transitional furniture reveal? A typical piece is a commode made by Roussel at the end of the period. The whole shape has become rectilinear, the corners are canted and the legs have a gentler curve. The front is broken, with the centre protruding. The *bombé* effect has disappeared. The marquetry is of such intricate and almost photographic design and execution and the bronze-work is confined to smaller areas. The flamboyant curves of the Rococo have gone.

Despite these changes, such as straighter legs for chairs and desks, the older styles did not die out altogether. Tortoise-shell and metalwork inlay pieces were still made in the Boulle style. The curving lines and 'plastic' movement of Louis XV lingered on, not least in the great *Bureau du Roi*, a cylinder-top desk constructed for the king by Oeben and Riesener.

In this period there also appeared a proliferation of small tables, some of which had mechanical devices. The *bonheur-du-jour* became more fashionable, and great care was given to its decoration. Other tables included *tables d'ouvrage* (work tables), *tables de toilette* (wrongly called *poudreuses*, a term coined in this century), *liseuses* (reading tables), and *tables à jeux* (games tables). And at this time appeared the first roll-top writing desks, called *bureaux à cylindre*. These became popular after the news escaped that the king was having one made for him by Oeben, who began work on it in 1760. This desk, which emerged as one of astonishing ingenuity and beauty, is now in the Louvre. If not the best piece of

Perhaps the most famous piece of furniture in the world. This *bureau à cylindre* was made for Louis XV by Oeben and Riesener between 1760 and 1769, spanning the Transitional period. It is now in the Louvre, Paris

This delightful *table de toilette,* of about 1765, is stamped L. Boudin (maître 1761) and is in tulipwood. There is some doubt whether Boudin made it, for he was also a dealer and sometimes stamped pieces he had for sale

eighteenth-century furniture it is the best known, and its history is probably better documented than any other piece.

It appears that at least six people were involved in its construction: Oeben, who mapped out its structure based on ideas by the designer Cochin; Duplessis, the royal *fondeur-doreur* who made its mounts, helped by Hervieux; and Riesener, who completed the work after the death of Oeben. The marquetry was probably executed by Riesener, assisted by Wynant. It was not finished until 1769, that is to say, its manufacture practically spanned the Transitional period.

The desk is opened and closed by means of a revolving roll-top, which is a quarter cylinder. This is made of slightly curved strips of wood linked together, which when motivated along curved grooving either cover the well or vanish into the carcase. This particular cylinder top is operated merely by turning the key in the lock.

The popularity of Sèvres porcelain plaques, medallions and panelling as alternatives or additions to marquetry was evident in the Transitional period. By 1760 Sèvres had become a serious rival to the Meissen products and a demand arose for its use as a decorative motif on furniture. Some *ébénistes* did not like it and would scarcely use it, but there were others who appreciated not only its possibilities for decoration, but also the financial rewards obtainable from incorporating it. A stock of panels and plaques would be ordered from the factory, each piece generally being signed and dated by the porcelain maker. These were used as and when needed, which meant that quite a number of pieces of furniture with Sèvres plaques are of later date than the porcelain itself, which is just another hazard encountered in the business of furniture dating. Martin Carlin (maître 1766) was one of the leading *ébénistes* to employ Sèvres porcelain in decoration, and a pair of Transitional *bonheurs-du-jour* completed by him in 1770 sold for 82,000 guineas five years ago at a sale at Christie's, then a record price for any individual furniture item.

The drop-front cabinet, because it occupied less space than a desk and also permitted storage of papers, etc., came into prominence. Its several flat surfaces, such as the doors inside and outside, the fall-front and the sides, gave the *ébénistes* much scope for marquetry and bronze-work. Again, this in turn justified the imposition of high fees for its manufacture.

Some of the pieces shown in the illustrations in this section are good examples of the mixture of styles typical of the period. No one method dominated until the very end, and even then

(*above right*) This *bonheur-du-jour* by Martin Carlin (maître 1766) was sold with its pair at Christie's in 1967 for 82,000 gns; a record sum. Carlin specialized in the use of Sèvres plaques for decoration. *(below right)* Sèvres porcelain plaque from work table, about 1785

the triumphant Neo-classical style was not so successful with *menuiserie*, and, in the author's opinion at least, Louis XVI chairs lack the grace and comfort of those of the Louis XV period.

No essay on the Transitional style would be complete without a note on the career of its finest exponent, Jean-François Oeben. Born in Germany in about 1720, Oeben emigrated to Paris and entered the workshop of one of A. C. Boulle's sons as an apprentice. There he received the best training available, and long before the end of his apprenticeship his gifts attracted the attention of Madame de Pompadour, the current mistress of Louis XV. She commissioned several works, which in time were brought to the notice of the king. Louis, whatever his faults, knew a fine work of art when he saw it, and when in 1754 Charles Joseph Boulle died, the king appointed the young Oeben to succeed as *ébéniste du roi*. For the next few years Oeben's works were confined mainly to royal houses or houses in which the king had an interest.

Despite his consummate skill and the evident satisfaction he gave his employers, Oeben did not become maître until 1760. Thus nothing of his before that date is signed. Indeed, as he died three years later, much of the furniture bearing his signature will have been made in the time of his widow's management of the workshop, and by Riesener before he became maître in 1768. Oeben was a superb craftsman who also excelled in metalwork. He specialized in making mechanical contrivances for his furniture, which operated secret drawers, sliding panels, etc. He was also a fine marquetry designer, preferring floral decoration to other patterns, and using native as well as more costly foreign woods.

In 1763 he died, aged only forty-two, and bankrupt, presumably because few people paid their bills, while he had to meet regular wages and costs for materials supplied. His widow carried on the business, with his senior assistant, Riesener (see page 74), who married her in 1768. Among Oeben's other assistants was Jean-François Leleu, who had hoped to succeed him but was to be disappointed.

Splendid drop-front secretaire in tulipwood and purplewood by Boudin from the late Transitional period. It provided great scope for his magnificent marquetry-work

(left) Transitional *encoignure* in sycamore, harewood and tulipwood, with marquetry of other woods, stamped by Oeben. Its shape suggests an acceptance of the return to classical lines

(right) Finely executed Louis XVI *bureau à cylindre* in tulipwood, amaranth, and marquetry, decorated with the arms of France, and made in about 1780 by F. Teune

Louis XVI

The Louis XVI style, which represented the triumph of the Neo-classical over the Rococo, can be divided into two phases, from about 1770 to 1780 and about 1780 to 1795. The first phase, which was well established before Louis XVI actually came to the throne in 1774, was an extravagant one. Although the superficial decoration of Rococo had given way to more substantial classical forms, with a noticeable return to architectural principles, heavy bronze ornamentation was still much in evidence, marquetry was as intricate and as beautiful as it was ever likely to be, and mechanical devices were still prominent features in a variety of pieces. An enormous amount of money was still being spent on furniture. Riesener, for example, was said to have received over £20,000 for one piece.

In the second phase, when France was beginning to feel the effects of the never-ending extravagances of the court of Louis XV, styles became much simpler. More home-grown woods were used in place of costly tropical varieties. Bronze-work diminished in quantity – and on occasions in quality as well. Marquetry was gradually edged into second place, behind the use of plain wood for whole panels. Court furniture maintained its excellence of quality right up to the Revolution, but elsewhere a decline began to become evident in furniture-making.

There was not a great deal of innovation in the Louis XVI period. It was an age rather of putting new shapes to old forms, of continued emphasis on comfort and practicality, and of finding new ways to decorate. But it was nonetheless a remarkable age, one which was notable for the splendid work of Riesener, and one in which over two hundred maîtres alone were working in Paris.

Among the principal pieces of the time were roll-top

desks, perhaps not as intricate as the famous *Bureau du Roi* but fine and costly all the same, *bureaux-plats,* commodes, and smaller items for women, who still exerted much influence on design. The drop-front secretaire continued to be in demand. A development of the Spanish *vargueño* (see page 32), this useful item stood against a wall, so the back of it did not require any decoration; indeed, some of those with the finest marquetry and bronze-work on the front and sides present the appearance of a packing-case at the back.

Bureaux-plats of the period became more rectangular, with straight legs. One, by Montigny (maître 1766) is particularly fine in its simplicity. Commodes had features additional to those customary in earlier periods. Some had three drawers in a frieze arrangement above the larger drawers. They were

Riesener was commissioned by Marie Antoinette to make this *secrétaire à abattant*

Louis XVI *bureau-plat*, made in a bout 1780 by Montigny. Its simplicity demonstrates the classical ideas of the period well

break-fronted, like later Transitional commodes. Legs were straight, turned, fluted and tapering, and were usually very short. The bronze mounts were restrained and heightened the lines of the carcase. There also appeared a development of the commode, the *commode à encoignure*. This consisted of a central commode section flanked on either side by an *encoignure*. There is one in the Frick Collection in New York, made by Roger Lacroix (R.V.L.C.) in about 1770, which has been described as marking the 'triumph of classical over Rococo.'

Menuisiers continued to search for the ultimate in comfort and elegance in sofas, day-beds, and to a lesser extent in chairs. The upholstery was as important as the carving and decoration of the framework, and a variety of materials were used: silk in a rich array of colours, velvet, embroidery (*grospoint* and *petitpoint*), moquettes (see page 41) and damask. Chairs were also made in more simple styles with canework seats and backs. Carved motifs took new forms, such as ribbonwork, cupid's bows and arrows, love-knots, classical features such as acanthus leaves, laurel, and a number of other

G. Beneman made this mahogany veneered commode in the Louis XVI style, with bronze mounts, in about 1787

designs executed to individual requirements. Woodwork was still gilded or painted, as well as left in its pristine condition.

Louis XVI chairs have individual features quite different from Louis XV and Transitional chairs. Straight legs, tapering, sometimes fluted, reeded or spiralled, descending from rectangular blocks with a rosette decorating the two outer surfaces, take the place of cabriole legs, although the latter did not vanish altogether. New types of back appear, the oval or medallion kind, first seen in about 1775, and squarer styles, occasionally flanked by columns. In 1780s the vogue for splat-back chairs which had been enjoyed for some generations in English houses began to encroach upon the Paris scene.

The arms of Louis XVI chairs with straight legs were brought forward over the front legs. They rose upwards and curved backwards into the back frame. The horizontal members were padded and occasionally brass-studded round the material. Despite the fine classical proportions, these chairs seemed to revert to the rigidity so common in much earlier furniture. Whatever else may be said of many Louis XVI chairs they do not have the same relaxed properties of the *fauteuils* of the Louis XV period.

In the last few years before the Revolution it became increasingly clear that the extravagance of the court and the nobility would have to be radically reduced, or national bankruptcy would follow (as indeed it did, in 1788, when Brienne declared the nation insolvent). This realization is reflected in much of the furniture of these years. Mahogany, widely used in England for forty years, now emerged as one of the commonest materials employed by the Paris *ébénistes*. With careful cutting, shaping and positioning, mahogany proved to be an excellent substitute for expensive marquetry, particularly if combined with metal mounting. At this time brass was used more widely for mounts. It was easier to work and less expensive.

Royal furniture, however, continued to have every skill lavished upon its manufacture, and Riesener and his associates were, right up to and even beyond the fall of the Bastille, making very expensive items, although they were finding it

Louis XVI style divan with fine upholstery and gilding

increasingly difficult to extract payment for their work.

Just as Oeben personified the *ébénisterie* of the Transitional period, so his senior assistant Riesener dominated the *ébénisterie* of Louis XVI. There is a kind of magic in Riesener's name, which is to a great extent justified. But it should never be overlooked that much work by his contemporaries was every bit as fine, in particular that by Carlin, Roger Lacroix, and Leleu. Riesener was born near Essen in 1734. At twenty he emigrated to Paris and joined Oeben's workshops, where he soon demonstrated the unique mastery he was to have of the art of *ébénisterie*. He became maître in 1768.

Twelve months later Riesener finished the *Bureau du Roi,* having inscribed his name as maker in the marquetry. It will of course never be known how much of the bureau was his work and how much Oeben's, but it evidently delighted the king who, a few years later, appointed Riesener as *ébéniste du roi*. Thereafter Riesener received the patronage of the royal

(left) Typical Louis XVI *fauteuil* with beechwood frame, carved and gilt *rechampi* white, made by G. Jacob, perhaps the greatest *menuisier* of the century

(right) Riesener's versatility as a craftsman is shown in this ebony commode with panels of Japanese black and gold lacquer, and extensive bronze mounts. It was made in about 1785

family for many years. It seems that not long before the Revolution his pre-eminence had been clouded. The treasury apparently requested him to revise his charges, and the king, meanwhile, had transferred his favour to another German-born *ébéniste,* Guillaume Beneman. But Riesener remained the favourite of the queen, Marie Antoinette, and continued to make furniture for her almost up to the year of her execution. After the formation of the Directoire he retired, and died in 1806. Riesener's work was a major influence on *ébénisterie* of his time. He was a versatile craftsman, especially gifted at elaborate marquetry, but no less skilled at the plainer designs. He also designed most of his own mounts.

The early days of the Revolution did not at first affect the Paris furniture-maker, who seemed to think that the crisis was only a temporary one. But once the king and the queen had perished on the guillotine, the old order had been swept away, and even the calendar changed, it was clear that the end had come to a unique period of furniture. Thereafter, cost was all important, until the emergence of Napoelon Bonaparte, when to signify his imperial power he initiated a new wave of luxury in the decorative arts.

Dutch Baroque rosewood and ebony cupboard on bun feet with two doors and two drawers, about 1660. Its internal carcase is of oak

The Low Countries

The Flemish part of the Netherlands, consisting more or less of what is now Belgium, was among the first regions of Europe to enjoy the advent of the Baroque style of furniture. This style, derived from the powerful Baroque architecture which originated in Italy and supplanted Renaissance forms, was not so much a new style as a modification of an existing one. It drew on classical ideas, but it was exuberant, with its emphasis on curved corners and broken pediments, and with a liberal use of scrolls, volutes, etc. It differed from the restraint of the classical in that it was dynamic, moving and exciting. Light and shade were used to create effect, and the ornament added made pieces ostentatious, sometimes even pompous.

The principal characteristics of Baroque furniture are ornate (and sometimes broken) pediments and twisted columns on large pieces like cupboards, carved cherubim, fruit and foliage on sideboards, etc., and chairs with bulb legs and heavily carved backs. The ornament is not new.

Dutch cabinet-on-stand veneered with acacia wood and other woods, of about 1690

Dutch lacquered doll's house cupboard, made at the beginning of 18th century, now in the Rijksmuseum at Amsterdam

Typical Baroque pieces in the Low Countries included four-door or two-door cupboards, sometimes with drawers under the main part, usually made of oak or oak-carcased with ebony and rosewood panelling and pilasters, and standing on huge bun feet, and wide chairs to accommodate the increasing number of folds fashionable in women's dresses. The construction of most pieces was rectilinear and somewhat limited, until in the middle of the seventeenth century furniture-makers began to experiment with bolder forms. Banding, rounding and chamfering became popular, and the contrasts between light and dark were accentuated. At the same time, as a result of the opening up of trading posts by merchant adventurers in all parts of the world, foreign woods, such as amboyna and rosewood, arrived in Holland and were soon put to skilful use. Indigenous walnut, meanwhile, was used for veneering, and a whole range of walnut furniture, which is part elaborate in the full Baroque style and part simple in the earlier Dutch peasant style, began to be made in quantity by a growing community of cabinet-makers who were to influence furniture design for a generation or more in Germany, Scandinavia and England from about 1640 to 1690. This walnut-veneered furniture was often extremely fine and has been much sought after by English collectors in particular. Many pieces were inlaid with ivory or coloured woods. With twisted legs, serpentine stretchers, bun feet and figured panels, it had a decidedly individual style. Towards the end of the seventeenth century, especially after the accession to the throne of William of Orange as William III of England, it supplanted the less attractive styles of Charles II's time.

At much the same time the Netherlands welcomed the new vogue for lacquered furniture. Dutch furniture-makers were particularly well placed to satisfy this taste because of Holland's widespread trading interests in the Far East where the style originated. They had practically a monopoly in Japan where for a long time the art of lacquering had been

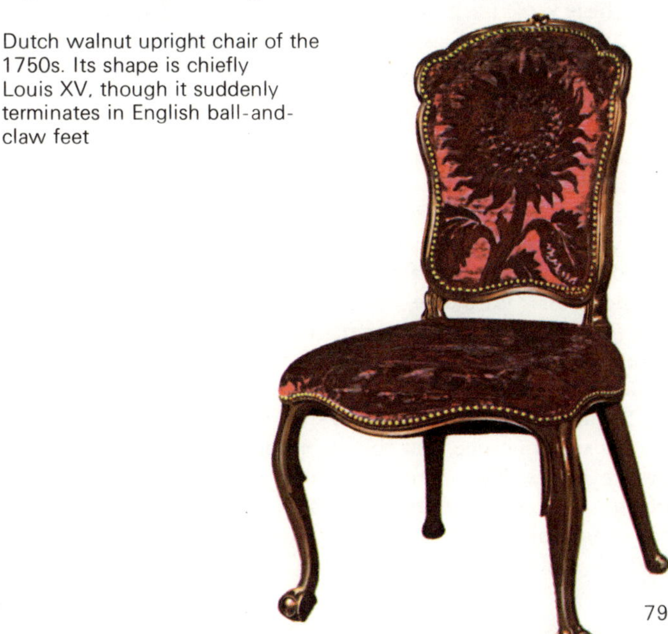

Dutch walnut upright chair of the 1750s. Its shape is chiefly Louis XV, though it suddenly terminates in English ball-and-claw feet

This splendid Flemish cupboard, made in Liège in about 1745, has a bow front, heavy Rococo carving on the doors, and paw feet. It is a strange mixture of styles

of an extremely high standard. (Japanning is the alternative word for the art.) They also began to make copies at home, and these were perhaps the best imitations in Europe, though the German work of Dagly and others was extremely good. The furniture styles in lacquer followed those of the walnut veneer vogue.

At the end of the seventeenth century Dutch furniture began to come decisively under the influence of France. The Baroque gave way to the freer expression associated with Bérain. After the Revocation of the Edict of Nantes in 1685 many Huguenot craftsmen had fled to Holland. One was Marot, a disciple of Bérain, who became designer to William of Orange. His influence was marked. Architectural shapes disappeared, marquetry increased in quantity and quality, often reflecting the Dutch traditional love of flowers.

Soon enough the eruption into Rococo forms followed, and in Holland Rococo fashions lasted long after the return to classicism in France. But they were often mixed with English native styles. The chair illustrated here from the first half of the eighteenth century is Louis XV in most particulars, but suddenly terminates in typical English claw-and-ball feet. Commodes, sometimes veneered in burr walnut, had *bombé* fronts, *encoignures* had curved mouldings, and cupboards had curved doors with heavy Rococo carving on the panels. Asymmetry abounded, and *rocaille* and shell motifs were prolific. The Rococo reached its height in the middle of the eighteenth century.

Eventually the reaction against Rococo reached Holland, and cabinet-makers turned to the principles of the Louis XVI style and adapted them to native furniture. A fine example of this reaction is a drop-front secretaire in the Rijksmuseum in Amsterdam. This secretaire is veneered in satinwood, ebony and a variety of exotic woods, with panels of Chinese lacquer decoration. It has gilt-bronze mounts. The Dutch continued to make commodes with fine marquetry designs, chiefly in rectangular lines. The Empire style was introduced into Holland when Napoleon Bonaparte set his brother Louis on the Dutch throne in 1806. Neo-classical ideas flourished, and mahogany with floral marquetry was the principal feature. The designs were relatively simple, with little ornamentation.

The pedestal table and upright chair in ash and amboyna of about 1830 are good examples of Dutch late Empire style furniture

Germany

The great Baroque palaces of Germany provided an opportunity for German designers and cabinet-makers to exploit their skill to the full. The fine decoration and furniture which survive from such buildings as the Zwinger in Dresden and Pommersfelden near Bamberg are a monument to the splendours of the age. With the entry of the Rococo style a new lightheartedness spread through designs for interiors and furniture alike.

It was some time, however, before Baroque furniture styles were fully accepted in Germany, and by the middle of the seventeenth century they were still a comparative rarity, especially in the North. But in Nuremberg the Baroque taste flourished and the city's example eventually encouraged the development of the style elsewhere. Small architectural

Dining table with extension leaves in oak, exaggerated twists to the legs, and heavy carving on the sub-structure. It is typical of German Baroque decoration

A craftsman in Hamburg produced this magnificent cupboard in the Baroque manner in about 1700. The carving is exceptionally skilful and makes the vast size of this piece more acceptable

details and scroll ornamentation were replaced by large pilasters, twisted columns and banded frames. Oak gave way to walnut, and design became more plastic and picturesque, with accentuated curves, stark profiles and elaborate foliated ornament. Twists and spirals were especially favoured, but they tended to be heavy and overpowering.

By the last decade of the seventeenth century German furniture-makers had reached a very high standard in woodwork moulding, planed or veneered. The Hamburg cupboard is a particularly fine example of this art. Cupboards were in fact one of the principal pieces of this period, as they had been in earlier periods. The columns and cornices display severe treatment. The ornament is extensive, with emphasis on

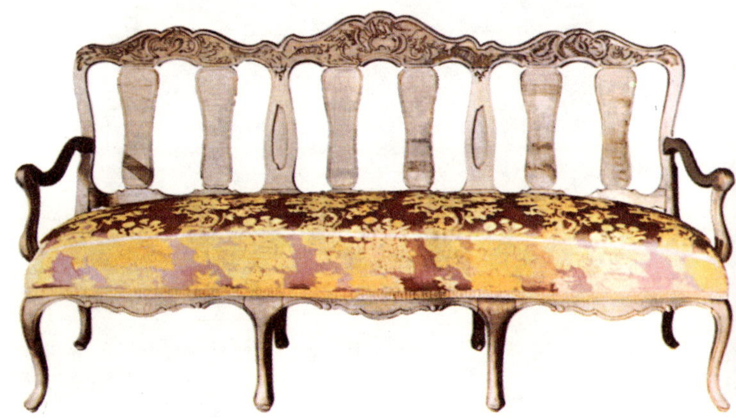

Abraham Roentgen made this carved walnut settee at the Neuwied workshops in Germany, which he founded. The style is more English than French, despite the decisive influence of France on European furniture of the 18th century

acanthus leaves, flowers, fruit and figures. Cornices are sometimes interrupted centrally by a projecting modelled pediment of exquisite carving. These pediments were sometimes broken, especially in cupboards made in Danzig.

A new form of writing desk appeared in Germany at the end of the seventeenth century. On either side of the kneehole and below the table top were drawers, mounted on four twisted legs on bun feet, which were connected by a gracefully curving stretcher composite. German craftsmen also took up the European fashion of lacquer furniture and used it extensively. In castles and houses, especially those along the Rhine, rooms were panelled from top to bottom in lacquered boarding, and the furniture in the rooms was decorated to match. A leading pioneer was the Flemish craftsman Gerard Dagly who moved to Berlin where he set up workshops and filled them with enthusiastic pupils. Some of these served their apprenticeship and then ventured out on their own to start up in business, notably in Hamburg and Dresden. The Prussian king, Frederick the Great, was particularly fond of lacquered furniture, especially if it was Oriental, and he commissioned a number of pieces for his residences.

In the third and fourth decades of the eighteenth century the Régence style of France was followed very closely by German cabinet-makers. Under such fine craftsmen as Effner in Munich and, later, Abraham Roentgen in Neuwied, German Régence developed in a more exuberant manner than the French, with its gay plastic motifs of figures, masks, Chinese dragons, etc. Chairs were high-backed, with smooth wood splats, on large cabriole legs. Some sofas used this construction as well, like the walnut settee by Roentgen.

In the middle of the century there was an abundance of pieces in the Rococo style in Germany. One of the principal designers was François Cuvilliés, a pupil of Effner, who pioneered the introduction of Rococo fashions in South Germany. The *rocaille* was lavish, the scroll-work extravagant, even by French standards, and quite often the most extraordinary shapes evolved. The commode by Bauer illustrated here is a good example.

By 1770, however, the enthusiasm for Rococo began to burn itself out and the Neo-classicism of the age took over. A leading influence was Abraham Roentgen's son, David, who worked both in Germany and in Paris (where he became maître in 1780), and in both places produced some of the finest pieces of the period in Europe. From 1800 onwards German cabinet-makers were producing plain and simple pieces, often in mahogany or pearwood, which have features more akin to English Hepplewhite and Sheraton styles than to furniture produced in Paris or Neuwied.

Italy

Italy was not only the birthplace of the European Renaissance, it was also the source of the Baroque style of architecture and the furniture that evolved with it. As early as 1600 the restraint of the classical lines of Renaissance furniture was disappearing behind exuberant ornamentation. Cabinets and tables, for example, were supported by painted and gilded understructures, with ostentatious carved naked figures such as naiads or negroes, or eagles and lions, jumbled up with scrolls, shells, cartouches, etc. Table tops were often surfaced with brilliantly coloured marble slab, or marble mosaic, or *piètre dure*. Chairs were richly carved and gilded, with greatly exaggerated motifs, and were upholstered in large-patterned velvet.

Some of the best examples of this Baroque furniture were executed under the inspiration of Domenico da Cortona, who supervised the decoration of the Palazzo Pitti in Florence and the Palazzo Barberini in Rome during the years 1630 to 1660. In the middle of the century the Baroque style began to be extensively interpreted in walnut, characterized by splendid veneered surfaces, with contrasting raised panelling or moulding. Pediments – tops, sides and fronts – of pieces such as cupboards were embellished with gay carved plastic ornamentation. In Venice, a leading home of fine furniture-making, the walnut was often part-gilded for contrast.

Venice was also the principal home of Italian lacquered furniture, which was among the best in Europe. In the period 1650 to 1700 this lacquer was usually black and vermilion, and the most general decorative patterns were *chinoiserie*. After 1700 the lacquer craftsmen began to use dark green and gold panels as well, and the total effect was very fine. Commode fronts and sides were gay and irresponsible. Lacquer decoration was later extended to a host of other household items, such as small boxes, trays, ornaments, hand

Three examples of furniture styles carried to excess *(top)* German Rococo commode of about 1760 by Bauer, *(centre)* Italian Rococo gilt throne of about 1730, and *(bottom)* Italian Baroque chair with heavy upholstery. The carving is over-elaborate, with negroes incorporated in the arm supports

This splendid example of Italian mid 18th-century lacquer-work amply illustrates the great skill of the Venetian lacquerers

looking-glasses, finger-plates for doors and even walking sticks.

Italian furniture-makers of the late seventeenth and early eighteenth centuries also specialized in various kinds of inlay work. Panels made up of semi-precious stones, known as *piètre dure*, and imitation marble mosaic known as *scagliola* work were used for table tops and fronts to cabinets. Consoles, always a popular item of furniture in Italian houses, were topped with huge slabs of indigenous marble, especially from Carrara, and supported by human or mythological figures or huge shells, often heavily gesso-gilded. They were over ornate, but in a large room they must have looked splendid.

French influence infiltrated into Italy in the early eighteenth century and remained a dominating feature for nearly a hundred years. Rococo fashions replaced the Baroque, and, as in Germany, the style was more frivolous and more pro-

Piffetti of Turin carried the Rococo style to eccentric lengths in this Italian bureau of 1730, inlaid with ivory and rare woods

When Empire styles reached Italy at the beginning of the 19th century they were quickly absorbed, to the detriment of Italian 18th-century furniture traditions. This desk by Socchi of Florence has little to recommend it

nounced than in France, especially in furniture from Venice and Turin. The inlaid ivory and rare wood bureau by Piffetti of Turin in the Quirinale Palace in Rome is a good example.

Further south in the peninsula the more restrained Neo-classicism of Louis XVI styles began to be reflected in pieces made after 1770. There were also distinct characteristics deriving from English furniture styles, particularly of Adam. By the early nineteenth century much Italian furniture had become simple and straight-lined. A writing table by Socchi of Florence is a considerable departure from earlier styles. It is in the Empire style and not very attractive at that. Marquetry-work continued to feature in Italian furniture, but not always to the best effect in rectilinear designs.

Spain and Portugal

At the beginning of the seventeenth century Spain was the dominant nation in Europe, but its power and influence were already declining, chiefly as a result of its fruitless political struggles with England and Holland. The enormous wealth which Spain derived from the Americas was not enough to balance the expense of its unsuccessful policies in Europe. Despite this, the monarchy and the nobility continued to live way beyond their – and the nation's – means, and they spent as much on their furniture as on any other artistic indulgence.

One manifestation of this was the extensive manufacture of such items as cupboards, tables, desks and the national piece, described earlier, the *vargueño,* (see page 32). *Vargueños* became the rage, and almost everyone of the upper class ordered one. They were made in the same tradition as the sixteenth-century examples, but as the Baroque taste spread from the Italian peninsula, in which Spain had territorial interests, the *vargueños* began to reflect the new style. *Vargueños* appeared decorated with plaques, gilded, encrusted with jewels, featuring marquetry, or adorned with architec-

Spanish Colonial carved wooden table of the mid 18th century, painted white and gilded, combining European and native Paraguayan elements

This commode, made under the inspiration of Gasparini, is a good example of the Spanish treatment of Rococo decoration

tural motifs. The simple sixteenth-century stands now yielded to exuberant Baroque forms, with turned bulb or barley-sugar legs, and stretchers in wavy form or in straight pieces were turned to look like a row of beads.

By the beginning of the eighteenth century Spanish furniture had lost much of its national vigour and individuality, and was looking more like contemporary French furniture. Rococo fashions were predominant, with weird flower motifs as a special feature. The commode became a principal item in most houses, made at first in solid woods such as walnut, with carving as a decoration, and sometimes gilding as well. In the middle of the century the Italian-born designer Matias Gasparini was employed to decorate the royal apartments in Madrid. He took Louis XV styles and impressed upon them his own individual boldness and gaiety. The commode illustrated is a good example of a piece made in his style. Chippendale and Hepplewhite styles were also popular in Spain, as a result of the close trading relations between the Spanish and the English, and the adaptations were often well made and attractive.

From 1580 to 1640 Portugal and her colonies in the Americas, Africa and the Far East were part of the great Spanish Empire. For much of that time Portuguese furniture more or less followed Spanish forms, but when in 1640 Portugal regained her independence, a great revival of architecture and art followed, of a distinctly national flavour. This affected furniture.

The Portuguese colonies provided the home-based cabinetmakers with a variety of exotic woods for making and decorating furniture, such as jacaranda, pausanto, huang-mo and various types of rosewood. Contact with the Orient resulted in strong Eastern influences in Portuguese design and the use of lacquer as decoration was adopted very early on. One of the main pieces of Portuguese furniture of the time was the *contador*, or cabinet. It was like the Spanish *vargueño*, but it included native features, in particular the absence of a drop front and the use of raised panelling on drawers, an effect generally achieved by using ebony. *Contadors*

Portuguese craftsmanship of the 18th century was of a very high standard. This unique games table, on cabriole legs, is in ebony with ivory inlay and the mounts are silver

were also lacquered with great skill in gold, red and green.

The long association with England led to the great popularity of English furniture styles in Portugal. When Catherine of Braganza, Charles II's widow, returned to Portugal in 1693 after 30 odd years in an English environment she brought with her a shipload of furnishings, including many fine seventeenth-century chairs, tables and chests of drawers, the latter being strongly influenced by Dutch styles. Portuguese furniture of the early eighteenth century, therefore, combined English, Dutch and some Spanish tastes, rendered in a national manner (for example, silver mounts were sometimes preferred to bronze). Portuguese cabinet-makers were particularly attracted to Chinese and Gothic styles, as interpreted in England.

In the middle of the century, as in so many other European countries, French Rococo designs encroached upon national furniture and the cabriole leg became a prominent feature, in squat or elongated form. The Portuguese still continued to carve wood, and executed some very fine work, as can be seen in the museums of Lisbon and Oporto.

Scandinavia

Scandinavian furniture of the seventeenth and eighteenth centuries is generally more derivative than original. The chief influences were Holland, France and England, and of these England was the most significant. This was due to the long friendship between the Scandinavian countries (they were among the first to become Protestant) and England, and the very substantial imports of timber England arranged with these countries, especially Norway. Much, then, of the furniture of these lands in the later half of the seventeenth century was but imitative of English styles, and these copies persisted long after the originals were no longer fashionable in England. The Norwegian chair of about 1715 shown here is of oak and it is chiefly in the style of Charles II; both had been superseded in England by this date. Here and there a small feature of national identity, such as a royal monogram,

(left) Mid 18th-century Swedish commode in deal, veneered with mahogany and other woods in parquet pattern. The design is Rococo but the feet are more English in style

(right) Norwegian armchair in gilded oak, of about 1715. The style is similar to that of late Charles II or James II English chairs

might be incorporated, or the carving might reveal Viking elements.

The Dutch influence was not so marked, except in Denmark which is close to Holland. Some of the Danish cabinet-makers of the early eighteenth century made chests with break-fronts in the Dutch manner, and their long-case clocks could have come out of Holland. Danish marquetry at this time was very fine. The English and Dutch styles, however popular, were confined to the furniture made for the commercial and professional classes in Scandinavia. The courts and the nobility preferred French styles. At the end of the century new royal palaces were built in Sweden and Denmark and these were decorated and furnished in the same manner as Versailles, although not quite on the same scale. French styles then gradually spread throughout the countries, and were found alongside English and Dutch influenced furniture in many homes.

The Rococo style was particularly fashionable in Sweden in the middle of the eighteenth century, and in some cases pieces of furniture were almost as grotesque as the German ones of the same time. Lacquer, too, enjoyed a considerable vogue and Swedish lacquerists demonstrated surprisingly high skill in this difficult art. Scandinavia did not produce highly individual furniture styles until the nineteenth century, and these are outside the scope of this work.

Russian 18th-century sofa in the Rococo manner, after a design by Rastrelli, who popularized Rococo but gave it an intensely individual style

Russia

Before the accession to the throne of Peter the Great (1672–1725) Russia was to all intents and purposes only semi-civilized. There is therefore little of interest in its furniture before the eighteenth century.

Peter the Great was the first Czar to bring Russia into the orbit of Western European culture. As a young man he had travelled and worked in disguise in England and Holland, and he had been fascinated by what he saw of the Western way of life. When he returned to his enormous kingdom he determined to 'civilize' his nobility. Furniture from Holland, England and France was ordered in great quantity, and in Russia it was copied as faithfully as skill would allow. Nobles were 'encouraged' to buy pieces and to decorate their homes according to the new trend.

The first pieces made in Russia at this time were in the Baroque manner, and these were in due course followed by Rococo styles, which in turn were succeeded by Neo-classicism. In all three styles, Russian-made pieces were often larger than their counterparts in Europe and their decoration was somewhat heavier, in order to fit better into the large homes of the St Petersburg and Moscow upper classes. By 1750 Rococo was the rage in Russia, and its prime sponsor was the great craftsman and designer, Bartolommeo Rastrelli, Russian-

This *bureau-plat* lacquered green on oak, was made by R. Dubois (maître 1754) and most probably given to Catherine the Great by Louis XV. Though it is French, it is typical of the style the Russian nobility favoured

Steel furniture made at Tula in central Russia was very popular in the 18th century. This chair, which is in the Victoria and Albert Museum, London, is finely decorated

born but of Italian descent. He designed and decorated the Palace of Tsarskoe Selo in St Petersburg in the 1750s. His work is very fine, but unmistakably Russian, grand, colourful and dramatic.

In 1762 a German-born princess became czarina of all the Russias, Catherine the Great (1762–1796), and she set out to westernize Russia further. She employed French *ébénistes* to work in St Petersburg and she commissioned additional pieces of furniture from the Paris workshops. Louis XV, who admired her, gave her many pieces, and one of these may have been the *bureau-plat* by Dubois, illustrated here. This piece, executed in 1765 in *Vernis Martin* lacquer, is now in the Wallace Collection, London. It is an early example of Neo-classical furniture from France. Marie Antoinette, Louis XVI's queen, gave her a *bureau à cylindre* made by David Roentgen.

Little furniture at court or in the homes of the nobility was original in the first half of the century. On the other hand, less elevated people did have indigenous furniture at this time, in particular a new and most unusual type made of steel, from Tula, in central Russia. This functional, and not altogether unattractive, furniture included tables, chairs and stools. It is essentially Russian in concept, but it also has some foreign characteristics, including Chippendale motifs. It is known that Catherine visited the Midlands in England during her reign, and presumably toured some of the iron factories where the idea of steel furniture was not unknown.

Russian craftsmen responded to the reaction against Rococo styles like any other cabinet-makers and much good quality 'Louis XVI' furniture was made after about 1775. Equally, the Directoire style spread to Russia, to be followed by the Empire style. Early in the nineteenth century, the Regency style of furniture of England held a particular place in Russian stately homes, and a considerable amount of ordinary, as well as ornate, pieces in this style were made. The chair shown here might almost have been made in London or in the provinces, such is the quality of its workmanship, as well as its design.

This Russian armchair of about 1820, veneered in birch, is strongly English Regency in style

Poland

The history of Poland has been as tragic as that of Ireland, and like Ireland it has had its ages of artistic flowering. Like Ireland, too, it has not failed to produce men of talent in times of the worst adversity. In the second half of the eighteenth century this was reflected among Polish cabinet-makers as much as among any other artists and craftsmen.

For a long time much furniture in Poland, particularly the provincial pieces, was heavy and ponderous, like the northern German pieces, and it was made of native woods with fine but typically country-style marquetry decoration. The decoration usually incorporated natural subjects; flowers, birds and plants. This furniture continued to be made well into the 1770s.

In Warsaw, Cracow and other large towns, however, eighteenth-century influences stemming from France bore

Mid 18th-century Polish cupboard on stand with typical native style marquetry in elm, dark oak and green-dyed walnut

Transitional style *bureau à cylindre* made in Warsaw in about 1780 by a Polish *ébéniste* trained in the Roentgen workshop at Neuwied

fruit in the furniture for the royal family and the nobility. The Poles were particularly fascinated by the Rococo, and Meissonnier is supposed to have provided designs for the interiors of many grand houses in Poland. French and German *ébénistes* were invited to spend time in Poland directing furniture-making in the workshops and were given extensive facilities. In spite of the directness of the French influence, Polish Rococo appears in general to be less gay and lively.

Poland was partitioned three times between 1772 and 1795, and the uncertain political climate, with its attendant economic misery, militated against the proper flourishing of native Polish skills, but many pieces of the times are nevertheless very fine. A *bureau à cylindre,* made in the manner of Oeben and Riesener, but distinctly Polish in simplicity, was the work of one of the Polish *ébénistes* who had worked in the Roentgen workshop at Neuwied, and then set up on his own in Warsaw.

England

The Age of Walnut

The Restoration of Charles II to the throne of England and Scotland in 1660 heralded a new age in Britain, which was to break away from the mood of asceticism imposed under the puritan rule of Cromwell and the Commonwealth. This was reflected as much in the furniture as in any other artistic field. Walnut, which had been used extensively for furniture for some time in many European countries, now came into fashion in England. Almost from the start it dominated English furniture and continued to do so for nearly a century. It replaced oak in solid form for chairs, etc., and it was also used as veneer on oak or other woods for cabinet-making. Some experts consider the walnut creations of this period finer than anything else in the history of English furniture.

Walnut has a natural beauty of grain, and it acquires a mellow colour and patina through age. When worked with skill it lends itself to the most complex kinds of decoration. Today,

Long-case clock veneered with walnut, about 1715

the walnut furniture of this period is extremely popular, but it is also very expensive, despite the fact that a vast amount was made during the century. Some antique shops in Britain have one or two genuine pieces, and one can often find them at auction sales.

Typical walnut items that have survived from the period in some quantity include chairs, bureaux, chests of drawers, tallboys, pedestal dressing tables and long-case clocks. But there are, on the other hand, comparatively few surviving tables, bookcases or china cabinets, probably because less of these items were made at the time. Far more common are oak or mahogany tables.

Walnut furniture styles in England after 1660 developed very quickly, and they were influenced by European characteristics, such as the bow stretchers for chairs from Spain, bulb leg and inverted cup motif from Portugal, and C- and S-shaped scroll-work from the Low Countries. English pieces were either walnut-veneered, walnut with marquetry, or walnut lacquered in the Chinese or Japanese manner. Architectural features were imporant.

One piece of the period which underwent considerable development was the chair, two examples of which are illustrated here. The Charles II type had twisted legs and balusters, carved cresting, straight stretchers and often canework seat and back. With the advent of the Dutch king, William III, chairs began to incorporate C- and S-shaped scroll motifs. Then the stretchers were joined to all four legs in a wavy X-shape. By the time of Queen Anne (1702–1714) cabriole legs had become predominant. At first these were joined by stretchers, but by 1710 or so they were standing on their own. Another prominent chair leg shape was a cabriole leg with carved knee and ball-and-claw foot.

While English cabinet-makers were constructing their splendid walnut creations, the art of marquetry arrived from Germany, France and Italy, in such a way that the English did not need to evolve their own type but merely learnt how to emulate the European. The English exponents proved to be very skilled, but they were seldom as liberal with colour or as gay with design as their European contemporaries. English styles were exemplified by jessamine flowers in white ivory

Typical Jacobean walnut armchair of about 1685, with cane back and seat, and carved cresting and stretcher

and leaves in ivory stained green.

The beginning of the eighteenth century witnessed significant changes in walnut furniture in England. Influenced by Marot (see page 80), whose originality of design had powerfully affected Dutch furniture, new styles developed. Pieces had decorative outlines, pediments, single or double domes, complete or broken arches, and scrolls. Doors of large pieces such as wardrobes and bureau-bookcases were panelled and not flush-veneered, and the panels were protecting or recessed. In place of panelling silvered glazing became popular.

Architecture continued to be an important influence and

cabinet-makers displayed a sound sense of proportion and detail. Cross-banding, which was the effective employment of cross-grained wood to produce contrast, came into fashion. Another innovation was the gilding of such pieces as wall mirrors, chairs, card tables, consoles. Looking-glasses became important pieces of furniture, as they were useful for filling gaps between windows or above heavy mantelpieces.

Most Queen Anne and George I (1714–1727) pieces, however, were straight walnut veneered, with or without banding or inlay. The carcases were of oak or pine. Mouldings were used to decorate simpler and more rectilinear pieces, appearing around drawer fronts or along table edges. New items appeared, such as card tables with folding flaps and special 'swing-out' bowls for money, bureau-bookcases with doors in the upper half, drop fronts in the middle, both concealing small drawers, cupboards and secret compartments. Another new piece was the bachelor chest, which had three long

This early 18th-century walnut armchair incorporating cabriole legs with carved knees reflects a considerable development in design

Walnut-veneered bureau-cupboard with double-dome top, and fitted with looking-glass panels. Made in about 1710

drawers and two short ones above, and on top a fold-over lid on which to write or for use as a dressing table.

After about 1720 walnut became increasingly hard to obtain. Embargoes were placed on importing it from Europe, and stocks of native wood were diminishing. So the cabinet-makers had to look elsewhere. They found a darker and closer grained variety of walnut in the American Colonies, and of course it was expensive to import. They also increased their purchases of mahogany from Spain and Africa which was still not too expensive to import in quantity. Its worm-resistant properties were already appreciated as well as its suitability for carving. From 1740 onwards the Cuban variety of mahogany began to be imported. Its grain and figure are superior to that of walnut and it was not long before walnut was no longer used as the major wood for cabinet-making.

Although this period has been called the Walnut Age, the vogue for lacquered furniture, popular throughout Europe, was enjoyed very widely in England from the earlier years of Charles II's reign. The principal item ordered by those who could afford this luxury was the cabinet. This appeared first in about 1680, but it was by no means the only lacquered piece of furniture. Other pieces included long-case clocks, secretaires, chests and commodes. At first, lacquered pieces were imported from the East, the best coming from Japan, but considerable amounts of fine quality pieces were exported also from China. The next development was for cabinet-makers to make pieces of furniture and send them to the East to be lacquered. Finally, at the end of the century they started to make and lacquer the pieces themselves. As the best pieces had originally come from Japan, the new art was called 'japanning'. English lacquer-work was never as fine as the

Queen Anne folding top card table, with carved knees on the cabriole legs

An innovation of the period was the small walnut bachelor chest, with a fold-over top that converted the chest to a desk or dressing table

A very fine example of early 18th-century English lacquer-work

original Oriental, for it was coarse, the reliefs were too marked and the coating was thin.

The more attractive qualities of mahogany wood as a material for furniture-making, and the growing dominance of French styles over all those in Europe led to changes in English styles from about 1740 onwards. The next sixty years were to be the most famous in English furniture history.

Four English designers

English furniture of the second half of the eighteenth century was dominated by four 'giants' – Chippendale, Adam, Hepplewhite and Sheraton. In a resumé of this size a brief look at the work of these men should be enough to show the very great heights to which English furniture rose in the period. But any further study must include examination and appreciation of the work of other extremely fine designers and craftsmen of the time, such as Kent, Vile, Cobb, Ince, Mayhew and Linnell, not to mention the creative work of a number of gifted and imaginative architects.

Thomas Chippendale was born in Yorkshire in 1718. By 1748 he was in London in business as a cabinet-maker, and five years later he moved to a house in St Martin's Lane, which he occupied until his death in 1779. St Martin's Lane was an astute choice, for two of the country's top painters lived there, Sir Joshua Reynolds and Sir James Thornhill, the patron of Hogarth. In 1754 Chippendale produced a book of furniture designs called *The Gentleman and Cabinet Maker's Director*. It was not the first work to contain designs for furniture, as de Vries and Ducerceau (see pages 27 and 30) among others had produced design books, but it was the first to consist entirely of drawings of furniture by a furniture-maker, and it was an instant success. It was reprinted the next year and again in a larger edition from 1759 to 1762, and it had a decisive effect on English styles for at least a decade.

At this time English furniture-makers were dabbling with Rococo designs and also with Chinese and Gothic styles. Chippendale adopted all three and modelled them in a sharply individual manner. He adorned his furniture with exquisite fretwork in the Chinese taste, employing it for the edges of tables, doors of cabinets, canopies of beds. He also designed –

Chippendale four-poster bed in the Chinese style, with pagoda top, now at Badminton House, Gloucestershire. This style of furniture was popular in the mid 18th century

and sometimes executed – chairs in the Gothic taste, with ecclesiastical-type splat-backs and top rails. He decorated some pieces after the French manner with Rococo motifs, combining shell ornaments with his own ideas. Principal pieces in his Rococo style were chests of drawers, sofas, china cabinets, writing tables, dressing tables and bureau-bookcases. They were made chiefly of mahogany of the best grain and figure, which looked marvellous after waxing and polishing. The styles he devised were often such that the ordinary country carpenter could emulate with little difficulty, even if without the exquisite refinement of the master craftsman. This is why there is so much furniture today which is described in sales and shops alike as Country Chippendale. It was copied in his time and it has also been ever since.

Chippendale himself appears to have made very little furniture, and only a few pieces can safely be ascribed to his hand, through bills made out by him to purchasers. The

Chippendale armchair in the Gothic taste

owner of Nostell Priory was billed by Chippendale for a table for £72 10s. Chippendale ceased to hold the centre of the stage after the advent of Adam in the decade 1760 to 1770, but, quick to see which way the wind was blowing, he accepted commissions from Adam to make furniture in the Neo-classical style, which Adam was pioneering in architecture and furniture.

Robert Adam was born in Scotland in 1728, the son of an architect. He and his three brothers studied under their father at Edinburgh. Then in 1753 Robert went to Italy to continue his training, and he fell under the spell of the new Italian ideas which derived directly from the recent discoveries at the excavations at Pompeii and Herculaneum. He got to know Piranesi who by his etchings had done so much to popularize the Classical Revival. Adam grasped the importance of relating interiors to exteriors of buildings, and when he returned to Britain in 1758 he had already formulated a whole series of new ideas of architecture and schemes of interior decoration. We are not concerned here with his architectural ideas (see *Architecture* in the all-colour paperbacks series), but in decoration he based his modes on ancient Roman motifs, such as strings of flowers, formal shell ornaments, palm leaves and disciplined scrolls of foliage. He produced a vast number of drawings, many of which are now in the Sir John Soane's Museum, London. They included a whole range of items of furniture, which were only part of the whole interior of a house.

Adam was commissioned both to design and build new houses and decorate them, and to redecorate existing ones. Among his important works were remodelling Harewood House and Nostell Priory in Yorkshire and Syon House and Osterley Park in Middlesex. At Osterley he commissioned Linnell to make furniture, including a pair of bow-front commodes in the Neo-classical style. Occasionally, Adam furniture was painted to fit into the general colour schemes of his rooms, some of which were executed by such distinguished artists as Angelica Kauffmann and Cipriani.

Adam chairs had new forms, straight tapered turned legs, fluted, reeded or plain. Backs were often oval within a plain wood frame, the wood being mahogany or beechwood. The influence of French ideas was here and there evident, although nothing displaced the predominance of Adam's own individuality. One of the finest emulators of his ideas was George Hepplewhite.

Hepplewhite is something of a mystery. His beginnings are unknown and his date of birth unrecorded. He learned the trade of cabinet-making in Lancashire and set up in business in London. He was active from about 1775 to his death in 1786. Two years after his death his widow published a book of his drawings of furniture styles called *The Cabinet-Maker and Upholsterer's Guide*, and it was this which made him famous. It was the first book of its kind since Chippendale's *Director*. It had nearly 300 illustrations, a great many of which reveal the influence of Adam. Much of the furniture is designed to be made of mahogany, with satinwood inlay, or marquetry in the French manner.

Many of Hepplewhite's designs were not unlike those of Chippendale's later years. These were less classical than Adam styles, and curves abounded, especially in chests of drawers' fronts and feet, cabinets, and chair backs. It is for chair backs in fact that Hepplewhite is best known, although

This bow-fronted satinwood commode, one of a pair made in the Adam manner by Linnell in about 1770, is at Osterley Park, Middlesex

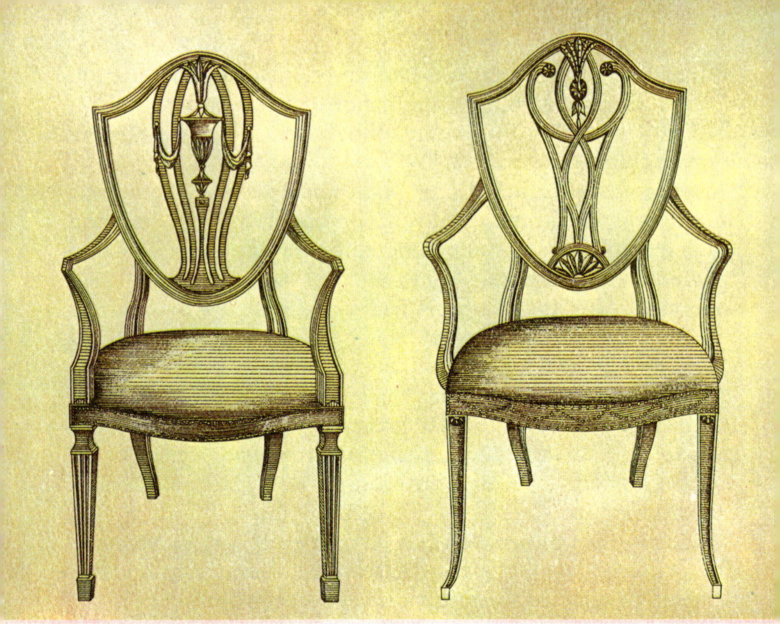

Two designs for chairs with shield-backs, from *The Cabinet-Maker and Upholsterer's Guide,* published by Hepplewhite's widow in 1788

Armchair designed in the Adam style for the drawing room at Saltram House, Devonshire, in about 1770. The ornament beneath the front seat rail is an unusual form of English decoration

he might well have wished otherwise, for his solid pieces are very beautiful indeed. Many different chair backs figure in the book, the most popular being the shield-back with a variety of splats inside. One favourite inside pattern range incorporated Prince of Wales ostrich feathers. The chairs have square or turned legs, the former sometimes with spade feet.

The variety of Hepplewhite pieces was extensive: wardrobes, with or without oval door panels of satinwood, with or without three or four drawers underneath; chests of drawers; sideboards in many shapes and sizes, bow-fronted, straight, or serpentine; sofas with upholstered backs and sides, or with backs formed by three or four splat-backs joined in a row; card tables with fine inlay or marquetry; Pembroke tables, with rectilinear flaps with rounded ends or serpentine edged flaps, inlaid or banded in satinwood. Not one piece of furniture, however, exists that can be ascribed definitely to Hepplewhite as the maker, and in his own time he enjoyed no fame. And yet, if comparisons are permissible, Hepplewhite furniture is finer and more graceful than Chippendale.

The last of the giants was Thomas Sheraton, a man of violent opinions and with little tolerance of other mortals, who lost his reason in the last years of his life. He was born at Stockton-on-Tees in 1751. He studied as a draughtsman-designer and journeyman cabinet-maker. For a while he made a precarious living, supplying designs to other cabinet-makers. He does not appear to have had either shop or workshop in London, nor is there any furniture that can be attributed to him.

Between 1791 and 1794 Sheraton published a book of furniture designs, in sections. It was full of advice and also of criticism. He considered that Chippendale styles were antiquated and that Hepplewhite styles had 'caught the decline.' There is no doubt, however, about the very high quality of his own designs, which were in many respects more original. This is abundantly evident from the many pieces of furniture that were made according to his designs in his time and afterwards. Sheraton preferred delicate furniture, which was light in colour, including painted pieces, and he specified that many items were best made in satinwood or other light tropical woods. His designs are straighter than Hepplewhite's and so closer to Adam. They had a strong influence on furniture at the end of the century, not only in England but also abroad.

Sheraton designed a number of intricate pieces, some of them for women, such as small graceful cylinder-top desks, dressing tables, work tables and games tables. The mahogany used was often brought into relief by light inlay or banding in satinwood. In particular, his chairs were favoured in most large houses. The backs were straight rather than curved, square rather than oval, and often in-filled with classical motifs. A series of six designs illustrates this theme.

One piece of furniture with which Sheraton is associated, but which he did not invent, was the Carlton House table. It is an unusual and very fine article, especially if made in satinwood.

Sheraton spent the last years of his life writing about furniture, not overlooking opportunities of criticizing both predecessors and contemporaries alike, with sustained impatience. The increasing instability of mind which in the end rendered him insane is reflected in his last works. Despite his very great skill and originality – and his high reputation – he died impoverished in 1806. And with him died the last major individual influence in English furniture history.

Serpentine-fronted Hepplewhite style sideboard of the late 18th century

Series of six designs for upright chairs devised by Sheraton and published in his *The Cabinet-Maker and Upholsterer's Drawing Book* in 1793

The Regency

The principal characteristic of Regency furniture in England was a revival not only of the classical forms of Greece and Rome but also of the styles of the ancient world generally. In this the designers and furniture-makers were not original; they were interpreters of older styles which in themselves had been classical. The furniture of the Regency period can in fact be divided into Greek and Roman, ancient Egyptian, Chinese, Gothic and even French schools of design.

The Regency period, like that of the Régence of France (see page 46), covers a number of years in excess of the actual duration of the Prince Regent's official term, and extends in the case of England from about 1795 to about 1830. Ironically, too, the majority of the aspects of Regency furniture were not in line at all with the Regent's own preference for Chinese fashions with brilliant lacquer and ornate gilding.

A prime mover of the Regency style was the architect Henry Holland who redecorated Carlton House for the Regent and Woburn for the then Duke of Bedford. He adopted French Directoire styles, and employed some French craftsmen who had left their country during the Revolution, but he merged the Directoire influence with his own interpretation of classical styles and the result was a great improvement. Bronze and stone pieces of furniture, or remains of these, such as couches, stools, tripod tables, etc., which had been found in Pompeii, were now interpreted in wood by the cabinet-makers, and the popularity of these revivals soon spread. The principal woods used were rosewood and dark mahogany, and these rich colours were accentuated by bronze or brass mounts or brass inlay. Pieces made were severe and rectilinear. Couches and sofas were commonly made, and so were sabre-legged chairs in the manner of the ancient Greek *klismos* (see page 11). Round-top tables on single stalks, known as monopodial, with huge areas of plain surface, edged with brass inlay, were in demand. Unbroken lines, reeding and fluting where accentuation of structure was important, and details such as lions' feet were major features.

An interest in Egyptian motifs derived largely from fascination with reports of Napoleon's campaigns in that country, and Nelson's great victory over the French fleet at the Battle of the Nile in 1798. Furniture began to display sphinxes in all sorts of places, at the tops of legs on desks and tables, as capitals to pilasters on mirrors and cabinets, and Egyptian carvings and hieroglyphics were reproduced along friezes under cornices. Some chairs were adorned with Egyptian heads forming complete vertical pieces from the arm to the leg top.

The Carlton House writing table was not invented by Sheraton but he produced designs for it in his books. This one is of satinwood

Very fine Regency rosewood circular table, about 1815, with brass inlay. The large undecorated area illustrates the splendid figure of this wood

The English never lost their enthusiasm for things Chinese, and in the Regency period the Chinese taste flourished, largely through its popularity with the Regent. It has been said that the Chinese style provided an escape from the five orders of Western architecture. Whatever the reason for its success, certainly the Regent had the Royal Pavilion at Brighton remodelled with strong emphasis on Chinese styles. The black and gold lacquered bed there is a good example of the happy mixture of Chinese and Western styles.

There was also a revival of interest in the Gothic style, particularly following the publication of George Smith's book *Household Furniture and Interior Decoration* in 1808, which contained a great variety of Gothic designs for chairs, sofa tables, canterburies and bedroom furniture.

It should, however, be stressed that most of the Regency years were lean ones, not least because of the heavy expenditure on the Napoleonic wars. As a result such luxuries as carving on wood, marquetry, or high quality gilding were rare. More emphasis was put on the woods themselves and their fine graining.

Despite the shortages, there was little limit to the range of

Regency sofa table in rosewood, made in about 1810, and now in the Royal Pavilion, Brighton

pieces made, such as sofa tables, a great speciality, dining tables with or without extension pieces, Pembroke tables, nests of tables, card tables, library steps, sideboards, dumb waiters, what-nots, canterburies, firescreens and music stands. Chairs showed a variety of leg styles: sham bamboo, lion's leg, plain and turned, scimitar, feathered eagle claw, cabriole with acanthus knee. None was so popular as the Trafalgar sabre-leg chair, so called because it reached its first general favour in the year of the great naval victory, when the back sometimes incorporated a rope design to signify the sea. Usually made of beechwood and often painted, these chairs were copied in one form or another for generations afterwards, and still are today.

Regency gave way to English versions of Empire, then Gothic and Victorian, which are not part of this work.

One of a set of six rope-back beechwood Regency Trafalgar upright chairs, of about 1810. This style of chair, with variations in the back design, enjoyed popularity for some time, and has been successfully reproduced ever since

Wales

For many centuries Wales abounded in native wood-carvers of the highest skill. They made not only the finest ecclesiastical furniture, but also domestic furniture of great merit. Then, in the eighteenth and nineteenth centuries the Industrial

Revolution, which in Wales resulted in the exploitation of a whole population as cheap labour for coal mines, iron foundries and shipyards, caused the ancient skill of wood-carving almost to disappear.

English styles of furniture of the eighteenth century made little impression in Wales until the very end of the century. Welsh people, prosperous and poor alike, tended to adhere to the native forms and to the native woods of oak, ash and elm. Considerable quantities of furniture were made, chiefly plain, severe and functional, but they were well constructed. Among the most fashionable pieces were the *cwpwrdd tridarn*, or three-tier cupboard, the *sidr fawr*, or the great chair, and the dresser, all three of which were exported to England and elsewhere.

Other pieces included benches, bible boxes, chests with

Welsh *cwpwrdd tridarn*, a distinctly national version of the press cupboard, made in three tiers. This is a late 17th-century specimen from Anglesey

Late 18th-century Welsh walnut settle with slatted back, from Carmarthenshire, and now in the National Museum of Wales, Cardiff (*right*)

understructures, buffets, courting chairs, bacon cupboards, double seats and desks. An unusual and very attractive eighteenth-century item was the slatted-back settle, usually made of walnut, with two drawers underneath the seat. Another was a clothes press fitted with a clock. One such piece was found which contained a copy of Bishop Morgan's Bible of 1588, chained to the inside.

There are few records of any exceptional craftsmen in these times, but it appears that the firm of Owen in Haverfordwest supplied very high quality pieces, while the craftsmen of Anglesey were regarded as the best makers of the *cwpwrdd tridarn* and great seats. It is interesting to mention here that in Wales the movable upright chair was being made as early as the twelfth century (there is an extant manuscript with a drawing of a judge seated on one of these while hearing cases), while the same type of chair was not produced in England until nearly the end of the Middle Ages.

When English high eighteenth-century styles did come to Wales, the pieces preferred were Hepplewhite sideboards, card tables, chairs and Sheraton tables. Mahogany was first used on a wide scale after about 1810.

THE NINETEENTH CENTURY

France

Directoire and Empire

The French Revolution, which broke out in 1789, did not put an immediate end to the Louis XVI period of furniture. There were still people about who were rich enough to order and pay for – or bold enough to order and not pay for – pieces of furniture from the many *ébénistes* and *menuisiers* who stayed in business. But by 1793, after the execution of the king, the demand slumped. There followed a spate of sales of the very finest pieces, in particular the contents of Versailles which were itemized in some 17,000 lots. The principal buyers were the English who obtained shiploads at knock-down prices. As it turned out it was as well they did, for it guaranteed the survival of a considerable quantity of furniture which might otherwise have been destroyed or have fallen into the hands

This pair of mahogany *bergères* of about 1803 in the Directoire style well illustrate the deterioration of imagination found in that period's styles

Directoire secretaire, decorated with lacquer panels and veneered in ebony, stamped B. Molitor (maître 1787) and dated about 1795. It marks the transition between Louis XVI and Empire styles

of people who did not appreciate its beauty or value. The National Assembly meanwhile also bought some of the lots and put them into the Louvre.

All the same, houses had still to be furnished, and so new styles evolved as the old were abandoned because they represented all that was most hateful about *L'ancien régime* – and also because they were often too expensive. The first new style was called Directoire, after the form of government that followed the fall of Robespierre, and it lasted roughly from 1795 to about 1800. This furniture followed basic Louis XVI shapes and designs, but with differences. Decoration was influenced by the painter David, the darling of the Revolution, and decorative elements incorporated griffins, Roman fasces, cockades and sphinxes. A general shortage of money in France

Empire secretaire of about 1810 in mahogany, with gilt-bronze mounts. The top falls down to horizontal level

forced cabinet-makers to use mahogany rather than rare woods, and marquetry had to give way to plain polished panelling and other surfacing. Chair legs deteriorated from the graceful cabriole or fine turned and tapered form to the square section, with lions' or other animal claw feet. Tops of chairs curved backwards. Frames were heavier, and the whole appearance was pedestrian and functional, no longer resembling anything of the past century or more.

The transition from Louis XVI to Empire, through Directoire, is seen well in the secretaire by the German-born Molitor. While the gilt-work is good and the lacquer-work fine, the piece lacks grace; it is heavy, stark and solid. When Empire furniture arrived in about 1805 it merely grafted antique forms on to basic shapes without much modification. Columns, cornices, pilasters, of antique design, were used as ornament on cupboards, cabinets and commodes. These grafts somehow do not really blend with the pieces. Considerable effect was produced by the contrast between dark red polished mahogany and fine gilt ornament. But the furniture of Napoleon's empire was designed for show rather than for comfort, and as an expert has put it, it was a 'pathetic and theatrical apeing of Roman culture.' Napoleon himself was painted wearing a Roman imperator's laurel wreath.

New items of furniture that emerged during the Empire period included break-front bookcases with lattice-work, glazed china cabinets, round dumb waiters, flower tables, and a variety of stands for tea. The beds were ponderous, and often sleigh-like. After about 1810 mahogany was not used for royal furniture in France, at least not in large houses, and beech, olive and lemonwood were substituted. Beech, when dyed, looks like rosewood and can be very attractive, but, of course, it is susceptible to worm.

When the monarchy was restored in 1815, the emigré nobles began to return to Paris. With them came a revival of interest in the older styles of furniture. The more cunning craftsmen and dealers, having secreted much Louis XV and Louis XVI furniture, now brought it out and offered it for sale. Many good pieces were also brought back from abroad whence they had gone in the early 1790s. But it was only the emigrés who wanted these styles, and prices were discouraging. A pair of *encoignures* with matching commode, stamped by Riesener,

Empire bed with elaborate gilded mouldings and pairs of decorative pilasters at each end. There are also light fitments

fetched only about £100. In his lifetime, Riesener had been paid thousands of pounds each for many of his pieces.

The Empire styles thus continued and developed, but after The Revolution of 1830 and the accession to the throne of Louis Philippe, himself a keen student of architecture and furnishing, there was a serious return to earlier styles, though not in the same degree as happened in the time of Napoleon III. French *ébénistes* began to reproduce, sometimes with fine accuracy, those splendid pieces that had been the wonder of Europe. Their other ideas were composites and many were very good. But there were also plenty of new styles, too. The *méridienne* illustrated here, made of mahogany in about 1830, is simple but graceful. This type of bed occasionally had let-down ends, and was the forerunner of a host of couches, chaises longues and sofas to appear both in France and in England throughout the century.

New techniques arising from the industrialization of France helped considerably in making the majority of this furniture very well constructed. Veneers could now be cut thinner and more accurately, inlays and marquetry were easier to prepare and put together, but the standard of design and workmanship correspondingly declined. Furniture was produced on a wide

The end of this French Restoration day bed of about 1830 can be let down. The piece is simple and functional, and not without gracefulness

scale – and often looked mass-produced. The individual touch seemed to have gone. Some of the copies of the old styles were clearly imitations, and many of them appear today in salerooms marked Louis XV or Louis XVI eighteenth century, because no one seems to know the difference.

An opportunity may be taken here to deplore two twentieth-century practices in connection with French furniture. One is the manufacture, on an increasingly large scale, of pieces purporting to be reproductions of eighteenth-century French furniture. These are so crude, so bald, so inaccurate in design and construction, and so lacking in any kind of feeling for the craftsmanship of the originals, that one wonders how they ever sell for the inflated prices asked and who buys them. The other is the 'gutting' of good nineteenth-century copies of eighteenth-century French commodes, *encoignures* or secretaires (even genuine eighteenth-century pieces have been known to suffer) and the 'building in' of record-playing equipment. This practice, which is sheer vandalism, is carried out commercially in Britain and the United States.

A fine lady's writing table with shelf, in mahogany inlaid with sycamore and lime, made in Paris in about 1835. This table is clearly in line of descent from Louis XVI styles

English copies of 18th-Century French Furniture

It has been noted (see page 124) that after the execution of Louis XVI of France in 1793 large quantities of eighteenth-century French furniture made by the Paris *ébénistes* were bought at sales by English connoisseurs and dealers. Before long, some of the Paris *ébénistes* abandoned France and came to England to make new lives. By about 1805 there was a good trade in reproductions of these styles as well as copies of Directoire and current Empire fashions. They were condemned outright by Sheraton and others (Sheraton also criticized the public for its interest in them), but to no avail.

By about 1820 the taste for eighteenth-century French furniture was fairly general in English upper class homes. Either the old designs were copied faithfully, and sometimes imaginatively, or the general features were adapted in new pieces. There was a vogue for tortoiseshell and brass marquetry, called English Buhl, which was encouraged by the Prince of Wales, and made chiefly by Louis le Gaigneur near the Edgware Road and Thomas Parker in Mayfair, but the productions were not always faithful copies of the originals.

Principal among the pieces copied at this time were commodes, encoignures and *bureaux-plats*. Some of the last were

This tulipwood *bureau-plat* in the Louis XV style was made in the 19th century in England. Close examination reveals the use of machinery

Teapoy in tulipwood and kingwood with gilt-bronze mounts and gallery, made in England in the 19th century in imitation of the style of Louis XV

most beautifully made and today would deceive all but the most knowledgeable collectors. In some pieces even the bronze mounts were initialled by the makers. It is also thought that some of the original French moulds may have been used in England.

In this time cabinet-makers also made pieces in the Louis XV style which had functions different from the original models. The Louis XV work-box in the illustration is in fact a 'teapoy' with a pair of lined tea containers on either side of a recess holding a cut glass bowl for mixing the teas.

These eighteenth-century styles have been consistently popular ever since, and the business of reproduction has continued unabated.

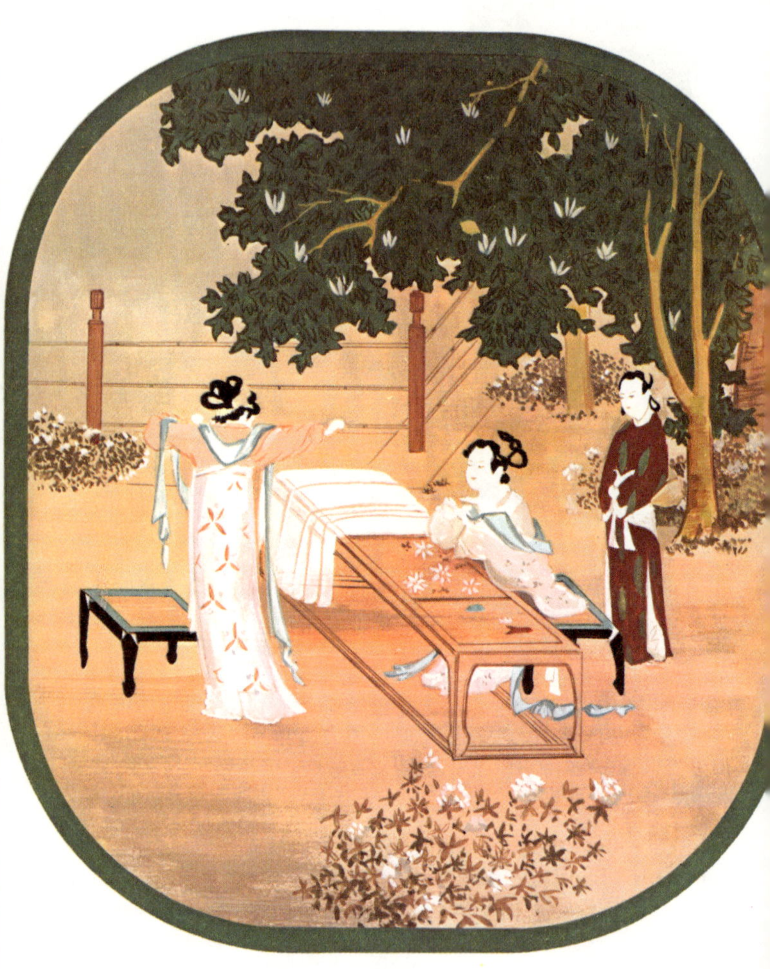

THE ORIENT

Advanced though most of the Oriental civilizations have been, the furniture of the East cannot really compare with that of Europe, except perhaps for the best lacquered pieces from China and Japan (see page 138). Over many centuries furniture hardly developed at all. In China, for example, chairs and tables made in the eighteenth century were often mere copies of originals from the great Han dynasty of c.200 BC to c. 200 AD. This is largely due to the very different manner of living in the East. Persian, Islamic, Indian and Chinese people did not need much furniture, for they were accustomed to sit on the ground on rugs for meals or in company, or at best they sat at very low plain tables, lying or sitting on divans or low couches.

What furniture they did make, however, was often fine and well constructed. Eastern craftsmen were particularly skilled at various kinds of intarsia, especially geometrical motifs in mother-of-pearl, ivory and wood, a style which from the sixteenth century onwards strongly influenced Holland, Portugal and Spain. China and Japan introduced lacquer decoration in furniture to the West and so initiated a type of furniture that was widely enjoyed throughout Europe for two or more centuries. For decades, various European cabinet-makers tried to imitate this work, with indifferent results, and their best pieces invariably included imported original Chinese, or Japanese panels as principal features.

The most interesting furniture of the East was Chinese and Japanese. Little has survived of Chinese furniture before the Ming dynasty (c.1368–1644) and what is known is largely derived from paintings and drawings from earlier ages. In 1600 the Chinese were still sitting on the ground or on low stools for meals or drinking tea from bowls on low tables. Seventeenth-century tables and stools had curved and scroll legs, or straight legs turned inwards towards the bottom. Between the legs and under the tops was sometimes a crossed trellis-like substructure. A development which caught the fancy of Europe and England was the nest of tables.

A painting in ink on silk by the Chinese artist Liu Sung-nien (about 1174–1230), illustrating contemporary Chinese furniture

In the Ottoman empire, which reached its zenith in the sixteenth century, the same living habits pertained, and one major piece of furniture was the Koran desk, found chiefly in mosques, private chapels and palaces. The Persians and Indians employed a variety of materials for constructing furniture and decorating it, including sandalwood, ebony, ivory and tin. They applied these to tables, chests, stools and cabinets. They also understood lacquer techniques and used these not only on wood but also on papier-mâché furniture.

The Chinese had a variety of cupboards and chests which often featured rows of drawers, with miniature cupboards. These cupboards were simple in construction with smooth surfaces, lacquered or inlaid or sometimes plain, rectilinear in shape, with occasional raised or moulded panelling. They were double- or four-doored, sometimes supported by an independent base, either box-framed or on short legs. They were made in a number of different sizes. Equally popular were chests on chests, which were either mounted on independent bases or had the base integral with the lowest part. These chests on chests were in two or three sections, and they had sliding or opening doors. They were often lacquered on the inside, and after about 1700 had metal mounts on corners and edges.

Seventeenth-century lacquer decoration figured landscapes with cavalrymen, or other human representations, in gold on black backgrounds. Occasionally, the effects were heightened by mother-of-pearl inlay. Towards the end of the century decoration became more colourful. Illustrations embraced houses, people engaged in work or play, birds, flowers, streams, the sun and the countryside. Red and brown lacquer were also extensively used, sometimes without any decoration, sometimes with gold or yellow landscaping and, later on, multi-coloured picture-work.

The Chinese chair did not alter much over the centuries. With or without arms, it was generally throne-like, with a stiff back and rigid seat. Some thrones were made wide

Turkish 18th-century Koran desk of ebony and very fine mother-of-pearl and ivory geometrical pattern inlay. The framework has been put together with great skill

enough for an emperor to sit cross-legged. They were usually square-shaped, with straight legs, square or turned, and with stretchers close to the ground. These chairs were functional rather than elegant. A mandarin's chair of the 1600s had legs curving inwards like an elephant's trunk, resting on a square-frame base. The sides were panelled, and almost as high as the back. The chair was lacquered in red with a solid seat on which had been lacquered an imitation wicker-work pattern.

Not all Chinese furniture was lacquered. Considerable quantities were made of bamboo, in conjunction with wicker-work of natural wood, or in natural wood alone. To some extent this depended upon the climate. China, like

Late 17th-century Chinese lacquered chest-on-chest. The inlay materials are ivory, mother-of-pearl, glass and hard stones

Chinese mandarin chair in red lacquered wood with engraved decoration, of the 17th century. It has a basket-work pattern for the seat and curving-in 'elephant trunk' legs

ancient Egypt, was poor in natural timber supplies, and needed to import it. Some wood came from India, especially sandalwood, known as blackwood but in reality a purple colour. One national Chinese wood with a reddish hue was *huang-huali*, and another, with a deeper red hue, was *huang-mu*. This latter is very dark when waxed and polished. It grows in south China and has a most wonderful colour. Camphor wood, which is aromatic, was widely used, especially for chests.

While the furniture and the decorative techniques above relate to the period c.1500 to c.1800, the secret of lacquerwork was known to the Chinese as early as 200 BC. But since the Chinese emperors did not have themselves entombed after death in vast mausolea, no relics of furniture of that time have survived. The knowledge of lacquer was passed on to Japan over a thousand years ago.

The antique furniture of Japan, like nearly everything else Japanese, was an imitation of the originals of another land, in this case China. The imitations began nearly thirteen hundred years ago, in the eighth century, when Japan first began to adopt wholesale the civilization of China. Several pieces of furniture of the eighth century have survived and are in the Shoso-in Depository at Nara, including an imperial white-painted silver-edged cherrywood low table on squat cabriole legs.

Lacquer-work was an ancient Japanese skill, and by the seventeenth century it was superior even to Chinese lacquer-work. Certainly the English considered it the best available from the East, for they labelled the art 'japanning' and described only Japanese work as 'right'. Motifs on the lacquer usually incorporated weapons, rosettes, foliage, and later landscapes, flowers, especially peonies, and birds. These were invariably most beautifully executed.

Low table, from the 8th century, on cabriole legs, made in Japan. This imperial piece is now in the Shoso-in Depository at Nara. It is made of cherry-wood and stands only four inches above the ground

The Japanese made a variety of movable pieces including chests of drawers, caskets, tables, chairs, in natural wood or in lacquered wood. The main characteristic was simplicity, achieved through consummate craftsmanship. Elsewhere in South-East Asia furniture closely followed Chinese styles, but here and there strong influences from India are detectable. A typical Chinese-influenced piece is the eighteenth-century cupboard from Siam illustrated here. The legs turn inwards like those of the mandarin chair. In Cambodia, few households had any furniture worth speaking about, and rugs and cushions were the dominant items in rooms. If rich houses contained beds or chests, they were as often as not made in China and exported to Cambodia. A similar situation existed in Burma. But Burmese furniture decorated with lacquer, a skill acquired there in the thirteenth century, was of high quality.

If there had been the demand in the East for the great variety of pieces that were produced in the West, and the styles and skills of East and West had been combined more extensively, some remarkable furniture would have resulted. An idea of what might have emerged can be deduced from the best early eighteenth-century lacquered furniture in Europe.

Most Siamese furniture was influenced by Chinese styles and this 18th-century cupboard is no exception. It is in black lacquer with gilt ornamentation

NORTH AMERICA

The furniture of the American colonies, which later became the United States of America, is handsome and vigorous, and in a great many instances, original. The first civilized settlers were from Britain in the late sixteenth and early seventeenth centuries, but they were not able to bring whole housefuls of furniture to the New World, and so they had to develop their own new styles in North America. Of course, these bore marked resemblances to the British forms they had grown up with, especially in their Puritan simplicity, but even in these early days the pieces took on peculiarly individual characteristics. What is more, they were well constructed. Some collectors have preferred American styles to their British counterparts.

The principal quality of American furniture was its simplicity, and this was to be its main feature right up to the War of Independence, 1775–1783. The first signs of change were after the war, in which the French had supported the colonists. The change was accentuated in the nineteenth century when vast emigrations from all the countries of Europe took place. Many emigrants were skilled craftsmen well versed in their own national styles.

Another characteristic of American furniture is that it was often narrower and taller than the styles it resembled. A third point was that the colonists were able to employ hitherto unused woods, such as maple, and they worked these with considerable skill.

More specifically, American styles followed the order of English styles, Jacobean, William and Mary, Queen Anne, Georgian, etc., and if one considers these English styles to be rich in variety, then the addition of individual American modes to them makes the result quite fascinating.

American Jacobean furniture was on the whole well proportioned. Made usually of oak, pine or maple, the range of

The McIntire Room at the H.F. du Pont Winterthur Museum, Delaware, illustrated here, contains Federal furniture, covering the period 1790 to 1810. The chairs are in the style of Samuel McIntire of Salem, and the sewing table is in the style of Ephraim Haines of Philadelphia

pieces was extensive, even in the early days. Court cupboards, like the Welsh *cwpwrdd tridarn* (see page 122), were developed from Welsh emigrant carpenters' models, though the decoration sometimes has a Byzantine look. A variety of chairs was made, including the well-known three-legged armchair and the spindle-back armchair, the two-row version of which came to be called the Brewster chair, after its supposed inventor, one of the original Pilgrim Fathers.

William and Mary and Queen Anne furniture was often painted (and later on lacquered), and the American cabinet-makers adopted marquetry with considerable deftness and enthusiasm, although the colours used were more akin to the English than to the European spectrum. Early in the eighteenth century Dutch influence began to make itself felt in American furniture (the Dutch settlers had already been in North

Japanned maple and pinewood highboy, made in Boston in about 1750. The style is Queen Anne, with Baroque ornament

American court cupboard, of about 1680, made in oak, pine and maple, resembling the *cwpwrdd tridarn* of Wales. Possibly it was designed by a Welsh emigrant. Its carving reveals, however, some Byzantine influence

America for some time), and this was manifested in the use of shell motifs, scrolls, broken pediments, executed chiefly in walnut. This influence was interpreted very successfully in America, even if grandiosely from time to time, like some of the early highboys (known as tallboys in English furniture) which had a huge shell motif in a prominent position at the top and bottom. The highboy of about 1750, in the illustration shown here, has a variety of influences, including English shape, fine imitation lacquer reminiscent of France, and Baroque traces in the ornament.

Some time in the middle of the century the new styles of Chippendale reached America, and they were swiftly adopted by leading cabinet-makers who, however, did not allow their own individuality to be submerged. Many pieces produced in the so-called 'American Chippendale' manner are exception-

American Brewster armchair, with a double row of spindles, made in about 1650

ally fine and are regarded as superior to the English versions because the dimensions are slightly smaller. One influential cabinet-maker who championed the Chippendale style and put his own mark indelibly on it was Thomas Affleck, an emigrant from Scotland who in 1763 set up business in Philadelphia and remained there for thirty-two years. Affleck was an extremely skilful craftsman as well as an original designer. He supplied furniture to many prominent people, including Benjamin Franklin whom he counted among his friends. A colleague of his, a man of equal accomplishment, Benjamin Randolph, also in business as a cabinet-maker in Philadelphia (1762–1792), was for a long time the leading exponent of Rococo, which he rendered in an inimitable personal style.

Chippendale styles continued to be popular right up to the War of Independence. It was this war in fact which interfered with the adoption of the Adam style. It developed in England at a time when the colonists in America were at their most angry with the home government over excessive taxation, lack of parliamentary representation and other grievances, and feeling against anything English was running increasingly high. Once the war was over and the colonists had successfully obtained their independence, a wave of new building fervour swept over the New England states, and since the old grievances had been resolved, resistance to Adam styles evaporated. Adam architecture dominated buildings, but so far as furniture was concerned, the Americans turned rather to Hepplewhite and Sheraton. A generation of new cabinet-makers grew up to design and produce a range of furniture which combined Hepplewhite and Sheraton with their own individual ideas, and the result was often extremely good. Among these new men was Duncan Phyfe (1768–1854), another Scottish emigrant,

American washstand from the end of the 18th century with tambour door in mahogany and satinwood. The tambour 'shuttering' shows Continental influence and illustrates the break-through of European styles in American furniture

who preferred Hepplewhite. This craftsman produced, among other things, sofa tables which match anything of the kind produced in Regency England. Samuel McIntire (1757–1811), an architect who was also a wood-carver and carved pieces by other makers, also made pieces himself. The chair illustrates the kind of work he did on existing furniture styles. Other craftsmen included Lemon, Sanderson and Frothingham.

In the early nineteenth century the furniture of America came under the influence of the Europeans who were flocking to make new lives in the new republic. Among these were one or two Paris *ébénistes* and *menuisiers*, and soon a number of French styles began to emerge in American furniture. Unfortunately, these were often of the Directoire and Empire variety, which hardly lend themselves to individual adaptation or improvement. But an undercurrent of English taste persisted throughout.

(below left) American version of a Hepplewhite shieldback chair, with carving by McIntire and *(below right)* design for a mahogany upright chair with a shieldback, from Hepplewhite's *Cabinet-Maker*

FAKES AND FORGERIES

Every kind of art has its fakes and forgeries, and furniture-making has had its share. But good forgeries are very rare, because the accurate reproduction of a rare and valuable piece of furniture takes a very long time, and so the field is at once a limited one. No forger can possibly afford to devote months, perhaps years, of his life reproducing one piece so well that not even the leading experts could detect its spuriousness.

There are, however, many commoner and less valuable items that can be copied with skill in very much less time, well enough to deceive the ordinary collector or casual purchaser – and, it should be said, a great majority of dealers as well. To steer clear of these fakes a few points may be helpful.

One thing to look for in a piece of furniture is patina. This is the word which describes the assumption, over many years, perhaps centuries, of a mellow tone by the wood through exposure to the air and light, and to regular rubbing, dusting and polishing. The wood has a kind of translucence that cannot be faked. It is also likely to be darker (or, if left in the sun for a long time, lighter) than the original colour. Polishing, with good pieces at all events, will almost certainly have been done with a mixture of turpentine and beeswax, or boiled linseed oil, and the effect is not possible by any other means. Thus patina cannot be reproduced.

The only way in which to get the required effect other than by age is to make the piece using antique wood which itself has acquired a patina that clearly puts it in the seventeenth or eighteenth century. This can be done by dismantling antique cupboards or chests and using the main panel sections or members. A considerable trade in old wood of this kind has been in existence for many years and some convincing copies have been produced, convincing, that is, to all but the handful of experts who really know what they are talking about.

A piece of wood originally used as something else and then made into a piece of furniture will give itself away. For example, the side of a dismantled chest of drawers of 1780 (dating proved perhaps by family records or bills or catalogue entries) used to make a card table top should show that the top is much too smooth to have been in use for 180 years or so as a horizontal surface which in the normal run would get polished regularly, knocked about, stained, and generally ill-treated. Some of these signs would show on a genuine piece, and if not, then attempts to remove them would equally be apparent. Forgers have been known to make these card table (or other kind of table) tops from sides of other furniture, and then leave them in restaurants or other public places in frequent use for several months, in the hope that in the time they would acquire the sort of wear accumulated in years of ordinary household use. But the task is not easy and is in any case seldom worth the return.

Furniture made in the eighteenth century and earlier was cut with ordinary straight saws. In the nineteenth century the circular saw was introduced and it cut wood much more quickly. But it also left unmistakable curved ridges along the cuts which, even if not at once visible could be felt by the finger. The forger generally does not have time to cut solid wood members or wood veneers by hand by straight saw, for if he does the piece will cost more than he could get for it. If, on the other hand, he uses the circular saw there is always the danger that he can be detected.

Another feature of pieces like chests, cupboards and sideboards is the key escutcheon. Leaving aside the possibility that the brass-work may itself be fake, escutcheons and backplates fitted 150 years ago will effectively keep the results of exposure to air and light away from the wood underneath. If the escutcheon is removed the wood underneath should be of a different colour to that of the rest of the surface. If it is not, then either the wood is not old or the escutcheon has been put on very much later, in which case the chances are the escutcheon is a fake. It would be very difficult indeed to fake the differences in colour sufficiently well to deceive the expert.

Nails and screws are believed to be a guide, but this is untrustworthy. Nails were hand cut up to about 1790, whereupon they were pressed out by machine. Wood screws were made as early as 300 years ago and had hand-filed threads with a shallow spiral. The screw had no taper or point and the slots on top were usually off centre. Tapering of screws is nineteenth-century. Yet both old nails and screws can be faked.

CONCLUSION

It has obviously not been possible to do more than just scratch at the surface of the history of antique furniture in so small a book. But it is hoped that enough interest has been aroused to make the reader want to examine more closely certain styles of furniture, and thereby enhance his knowledge of them, especially those which he may wish to start collecting.

In the field of antique furniture – and indeed of all antiques – there are perhaps more opportunities for sharp dealing than in any other field of merchandise, and so the more knowledge ordinary people can acquire about the history of antique furniture, the makers, the styles and the techniques of manufacture, the better they may be protected. While it takes years to become an expert in any one field, I am inclined to think that 'a little learning' in the antique field is not so dangerous a thing as it may be elsewhere.

To this end it may be helpful to mention some places where various styles of furniture can be studied at first hand. A large selection of eighteenth-century French furniture can be seen at Waddesdon Manor, near Aylesbury, which is administered by the National Trust, at the Victoria and Albert Museum in London, at Osterley Park in Middlesex, and at the Brighton Art Gallery and Museum. The finest collection, however, is the Wallace Collection, housed in Manchester Square, London, the director of which is probably the leading authority on French furniture in the world.

There are many good collections of English furniture in the United Kingdom. The Victoria and Albert Museum has a most comprehensive range from late Medieval to late Georgian; so has the Geffrye Museum in East London. Adam designs can be studied at Osterley Park, at Kenwood House, London, at Kedleston Hall, Derbyshire, and at Harewood House, near Leeds (which also has Chippendale furniture). Some Sheraton designs may be seen at the Royal Pavilion in Brighton.

Welsh furniture is well worth further study, as few people have troubled to familiarize themselves with the native styles and craftsmanship. Good collections can be visited at the National Museum of Wales in Cardiff, at the Museum of Welsh Antiquities in Bangor and at Gwydir Castle at Llanrwst.

WOODS USED BY FURNITURE MAKERS

EBONY: hard, black, with fine grain, often used for inlay ▶

◀ OBECHE: unusual tropical African; hard, white to pale-yellow

WALNUT: pale brown, very good for veneer; principal wood of 17th C. ▶

◀ ROSEWOOD: hardwood from S. America, India; dark purple-brown, known also as kingwood

OAK: coarse grained hard wood; main wood used up to 17th C. ▶

◀ MAPLE: fine grained pale brown, commonly used in North America

TULIPWOOD: reddish striped, used widely for veneers in French 18th C. furniture ▶

◀ PINEWOOD: soft, red to yellow, used for carcases of pieces or country furniture; also known as deal

SYCAMORE: very white fine grain wood, good for veneers ▶

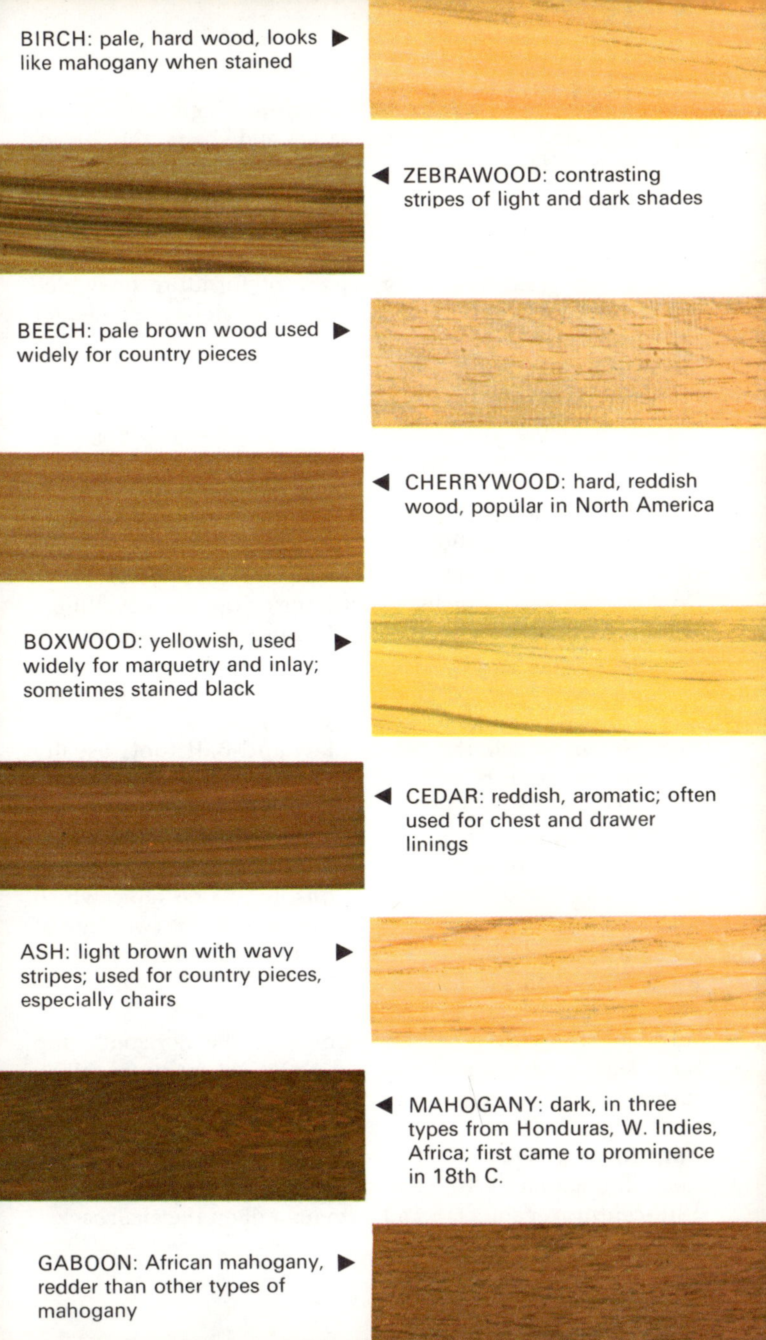
BIRCH: pale, hard wood, looks like mahogany when stained
ZEBRAWOOD: contrasting stripes of light and dark shades
BEECH: pale brown wood used widely for country pieces
CHERRYWOOD: hard, reddish wood, popular in North America
BOXWOOD: yellowish, used widely for marquetry and inlay; sometimes stained black
CEDAR: reddish, aromatic; often used for chest and drawer linings
ASH: light brown with wavy stripes; used for country pieces, especially chairs
MAHOGANY: dark, in three types from Honduras, W. Indies, Africa; first came to prominence in 18th C.
GABOON: African mahogany, redder than other types of mahogany

GLOSSARY

Apron, a band of wood, with or without a drawer, under a table top

Banding, ornamental border of a furniture surface, made of a colour, grain or type of wood different from the wood of the surface

Bevelling, flattening of a corner of a square or rectangular section of wood. Also known as canting or chamfering

Bow front, convex fronting to furniture, especially that of the 18th century and after. Bow-fronted pieces included chests of drawers and corner cupboards

Break front, term describing the construction of a piece of furniture in which the central portion projects beyond the remainder of the piece

Broken pediment, a typical Baroque form of ornament for buildings and furniture. The apex of the pediment is missing

Bulb leg, a phrase used to describe late Renaissance or subsequent styles of furniture legs where these are turned inwards creating a bulb shape

Bun foot, a squashed ball foot, found on 17th- and 18th-century cabinets and chests

Cabriole leg, usually on tables and chairs, this curves out on the downward path and then curves inwards, tapering at the same time

Carcase, the body of any piece of furniture on which veneers of wood are glued for surface decoration

Cartouche, a decorative motif on furniture or bronze in which usually, though not always, a coat of arms is portrayed in carving

Caryatid, a sculptured figure of a woman used as a support on a piece of furniture

Chamfering, see Bevelling

Chinoiserie, decorative artwork which has Chinese characteristics, such as pagodas or fretwork

Claw-and-ball foot, usually at the end of a cabriole leg, this represents a bird's talons (or a lion's paw) clutching a sphere

Console, a side table which rests on one or two legs at the front but which needs to be affixed to the wall at the back for support

Cornice, the horizontal top of a piece of furniture which projects forwards, such as on a bureau-bookcase or tallboy

Cresting rail, as applied to a chair, the uppermost horizontal rail on the chairback

Crossbanding, banding of wood whose grain is generally at right angles to the direction of the grain of the principal wood surface.

Cylinder-top desk, a desk the main operative parts of which are enclosed by a quarter-cylinder of wood which moves upwards or downwards to open or close the desk. The upward movement takes the cylinder into the carcase of the desk

Dentil cornice, a cornice with a form of decorative moulding consisting of cubes of wood spaced out regularly in a row

Dovetailing, a method of joining two pieces of wood together at right angles by means of affixing fan-shaped projections at the end of one member into fan-shaped slots at the end of the other

Dowel, a wooden pin without a head, used in joining wood members

Escutcheon, the bronze or brass plate over a keyhole

Fluting, a form of decoration in which concave grooves are cut into the wood, in rows close together or separated

Fretwork, woodcarving in patterns of straight lines, either open or as raised moulding on surfaces. This is a feature of the Chinese taste

Frieze, the strip of wood below the cornice on a piece of furniture. This may be decorated with fretwork or inlay or gilt-bronze mounting

Gesso, a form of decoration in relief. The motif is modelled in size and plaster or whiting and then surfaced with gold leaf (or gold paint in imitations). Typical 'gesso' pieces are looking-glasses, consoles and picture frames

Grain, the lines of the fibre in wood which give a pattern (see the section on Woods for examples)

Grotesque, decorative sculpture on wood with fantastic interweaving of human and animal forms, sometimes with foliage

Lacquering, process of applying several layers of paint and special varnish to produce a decorated surface

Linenfold, type of woodcarving representing folded linen. It was used in both Gothic and early Renaissance periods especially on panelling on Flemish and English pieces

Long-case clock, correct term for 'grandfather' or 'grandmother' clock

Marquetry, a development of intarsia. It is inlay-work of veneers of woods of different colours and grains in delicate patterns

Mortise and tenon, one of the main forms of joining wood members. The end of one member has a rectangular section slot into which a similar rectangular section recessed projection fits. The two are glued or affixed by means of dowels

Moulding, a shaped member such as that used to enclose panels on cupboards, or a shaped edge of a table top, pediment or cornice, etc.

Mounts, gilt-bronze, bronze or brass sculpture affixed to corners, edges and other surfaces of furniture, chiefly for decoration

Over-stuffed seat, a chair seat in which the upholstery is carried over and underneath the seat rails

Parquetry, wood inlay pattern made up from wood of the same colour but different grain configuration. The patterns are usually geometric

Patina, a surface on wood (and on some metals) produced by age and contributed to by generations of polishing and use

Pediment, a triangular structure on the top of certain items of furniture, like some long-case clocks and some cabinets

Pilaster, a rectangular column, particularly one which forms an abutment on a wall or panel

Plinth, the base of certain items where this base has a solid square-shaped form, such as a dressoir

Réchampi, decoration in relief, gilded or painted in different tones, or produced by a combination of both

Reeding, form of wood decoration of convex mouldings adjacent in rows, either as surfacing for a turned leg or as ornament on flat surfaces

Ribbonwork, decoration in wood or plaster in the form of ribbons and bows

Roll-top desk, similar to cylinder-top desk, but in this case the quarter cylinder is constructed of slats of wood and not of one whole piece

Sabot, bronze or brass hollow sculpture in the shape of a foot, fitted over the end of a table leg

Scagliola work, imitation marble, made up from fine quality plaster and decorated. It can be highly polished.

Scrollwork, decoration in wood, plaster or bronze, shaped like a scroll; term often used to define any spiral or flowing lines in furniture decoration

Serpentine, form of shaping to fronts or surface edges of certain pieces of furniture, in which the ends curve inwards to meet the centre section which curves outwards

Settle, a chest with a back part rising from the rear panel, with arms protruding, to provide a seat. The seat top lifts so that the chest can be used for storage

Silvered glazing, glazing of a cupboard with mirror glass

Sofa table, rectangular table, often with two drawers in one line and with a flap at each end. The central part is supported by a bracket at each end connected at the bottom by a stretcher. Intended for women to use at sofas

Spade foot, square tapering section foot of a table or chair leg. Its greatest dimension is a little larger than that of the leg where the foot begins

Splat-back, a splat is a panel of wood slotted between the back seat rail and the cresting rail of an upright chair

Stretcher, a member of wood shaped and fitted between the legs of a chair or table for strength

Surmount, term for a shaped marble slab placed on top of some types of cabinet furniture such as commodes, encoignures, etc.

Swash turning, otherwise called 'barley sugar twisting', a form of woodturning particularly popular in the second half of the seventeenth century

Turning, method of producing legs, pillars, etc., on furniture. Wood was turned on a pole-lathe. Various kinds of turning were popular, including twisting like a barley-sugar stick, or shaping like a row of beads

Veneer, a thin layer of wood, originally cut by hand, but by machine after the early 19th century, used to surface or decorate the carcase of a piece of furniture

Vernis Martin, the special lacquer patented by the Martin brothers in France in 1730. It was a coloured varnish applied in many coats and rubbed down to produce a fine lustre. Many colours were used, but the most popular was green

Volute, a spiral scroll characteristic of Ionic and Corinthian capitals in architecture, and applied to furniture decoration, especially in Baroque styles

BOOKS TO READ

A great many books on antique furniture have been written in the past two hundred years. Unfortunately, the proportion of useful ones to the total is small, and the list below contains some of the most authoritative and informative of them.

The Connoisseur's Complete Period Guides. London, 1968.

Victoria and Albert Museum. *Chests of Drawers and Commodes.* H.M.S.O., London, 1960.

Victoria and Albert Museum. *Tables.* H.M.S.O., London, 1961.

World Furniture edited by Helena Hayward. Hamlyn, London, 1967.

The Age of Louis XV by A. G. Palacios. Hamlyn, London, 1969.

The Age of Louis XVI by A. G. Palacios. Hamlyn, London, 1969.

Paris Furniture by Charles Packer. Ceramic Book Co., Newport, Monmouthshire, 1956.

Louis XVI Furniture by F. J. B. Watson. Alec Tiranti, London, 1961.

Encyclopedia of Furniture by H. Schmitz. Benn Bros., London, 1926.

The Art of Furniture by O. Wanscher. Allen & Unwin, London, 1968.

The Dictionary of English Furniture by P. Macquoid and R. Edwards. Revised by R. Edwards. Country Life, London, 1964.

Chippendale's The Gentleman and Cabinet-maker's Director, 1754. Reprinted by Dover Publications Inc., New York, 1966.

Hepplewhite's Cabinet-Maker and Upholsterer's Guide, 1788.

Sheraton's Cabinet-Maker & Upholsterer's Drawing Book, 1791–4.

Georgian cabinet-makers by R. Edwards and M. Jourdain. Revised edition. Country Life, London, 1955.

Regency Furniture by M. Jourdain. Revised by R. Edwards. Country Life, London, 1965.

French Eighteenth Century Furniture by G. Souchal. Weidenfeld & Nicolson, London, 1961.

English 18th century furniture by D. Nickerson. Weidenfeld & Nicolson, London, 1963.

English furniture designs of the eighteenth century by P. Ward-Jackson. Victoria and Albert Museum, London, 1959.

American Antique Furniture by E. G. Miller. Constable, London, 1967.

History of English Furniture (4 vols.) by P. Macquoid. Lawrence & Bullon, London, 1905–8.

English Furniture of the Eighteenth Century (3 vols.) by H. Cescinsky. G. Routledge & Sons, London, 1911–12.

French Furniture & Interior Decoration of the 18th Century. Barrie & Rockliff, London, 1967.

Italian Furniture & Interiors by G. L. Hunter. Batsford, London, 1920.

INDEX

Page numbers in **bold** type refer to illustrations

SOME OTHER TITLES IN THIS SERIES

Arts — General Information
Domestic Animals and Pets — History and Mythology
Domestic Science — Natural History
Gardening — Popular Science

Arts
Antique Furniture/Architecture/Clocks and Watches/Glass for Collectors/Jewellery/Musical Instruments/Porcelain/Pottery/Victoriana

Domestic Animals and Pets
Budgerigars/Cats/Dog Care/Dogs/Horses and Ponies/Pet Birds/Pets for Children/Tropical Freshwater Aquaria/Tropical Marine Aquaria

Domestic Science
Flower Arranging

Gardening
Chrysanthemums/Garden Flowers/Garden Shrubs/House Plants/Plants for Small Gardens/Roses

General Information
Aircraft/Arms and Armour/Coins and Medals/Flags/ Fortune Telling/Freshwater Fishing/Guns/Military Uniforms/Motor Boats and Boating/National Costumes of the world/ Orders and Decorations/Rockets and Missiles/ Sailing/Sailing Ships and Sailing Craft/Sea Fishing/Trains/Veteran and Vintage Cars/Warships

History and Mythology
Age of Shakespeare/Archaeology/Discovery of: Africa/ The American West/Australia/Japan/North America/South America/Great Land Battles/Great Naval Battles/Myths and Legends of: Africa/Ancient Egypt/Ancient Greece/Ancient Rome/India/The South Seas/Witchcraft and Black Magic

Natural History
The Animal Kingdom/Animals of Australia and New Zealand/Animals of Southern Asia/Bird Behaviour/Birds of Prey/Butterflies/Evolution of Life/Fishes of the world/ Fossil Man/A Guide to the Seashore/Life in the Sea/Mammals of the World/Monkeys and Apes/Natural History Collecting/The Plant Kingdom/Prehistoric Animals/Seabirds/Seashells/Snakes of the world/Trees of the world/Tropical Birds/Wild Cats

Popular Science
Astronomy/Atomic Energy/Chemistry/Computers at Work/ The Earth/Electricity/Electronics/Exploring the Planets/Heredity
The Human Body/Mathematics/Microscopes and Microscopic Life/Physics/Undersea Exploration/The Weather Guide